ADULT COLORING BOOK

KEEP CALM AND STRESS DOWN

DESIGN FLOWERS, ANIMAL, SUN, PATTERN

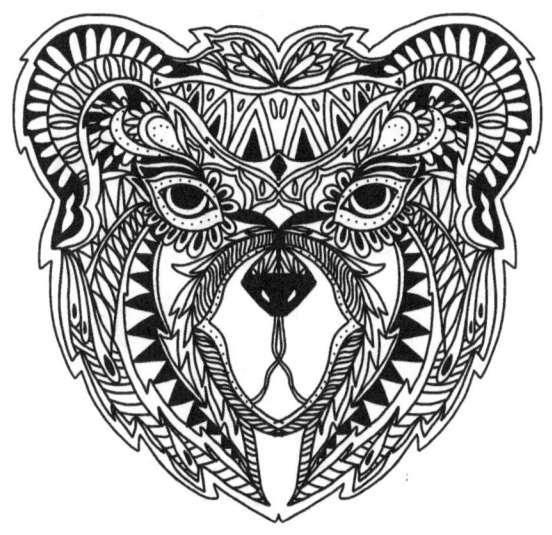

THIS BOOK BELONGS TO

....

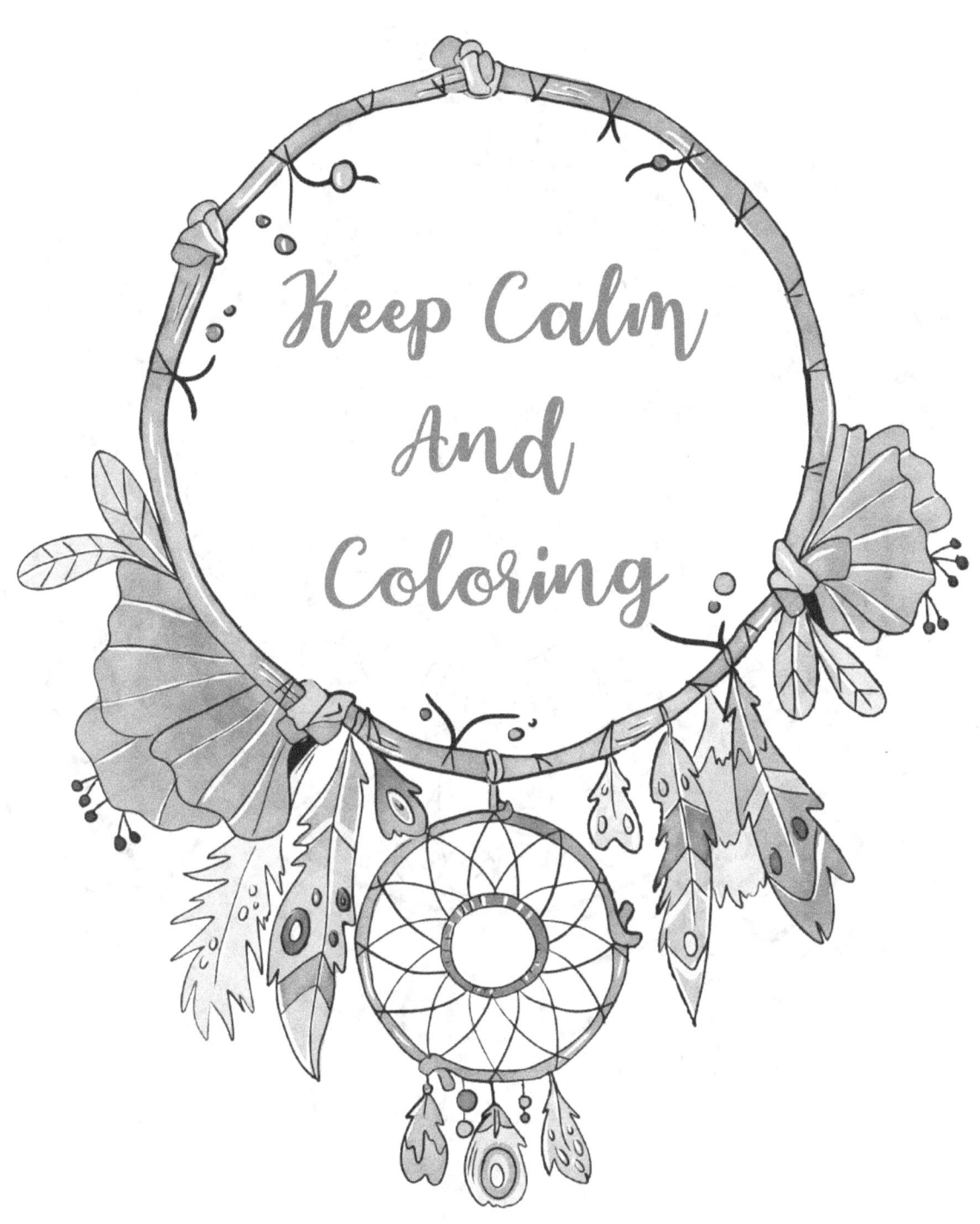

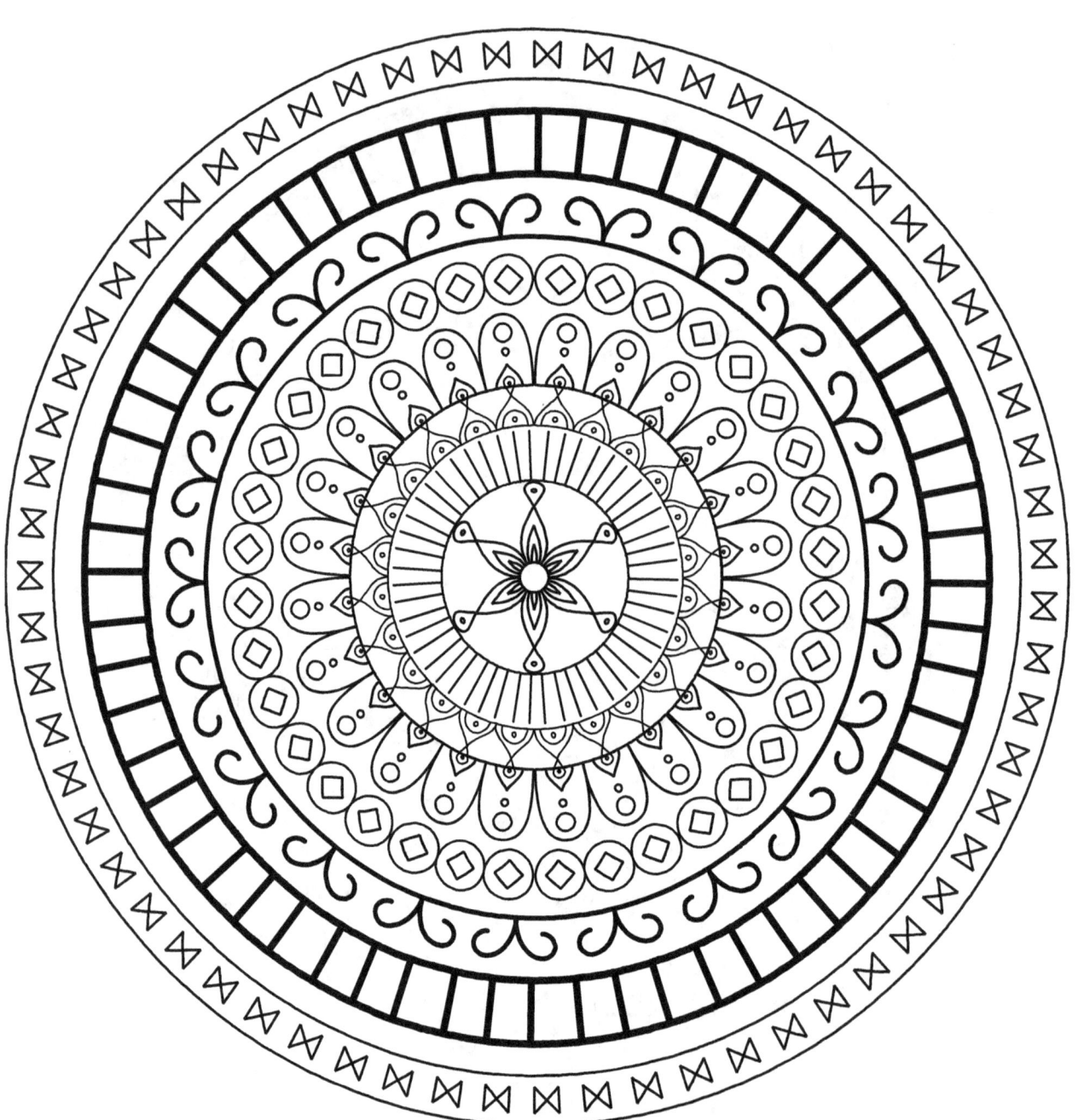

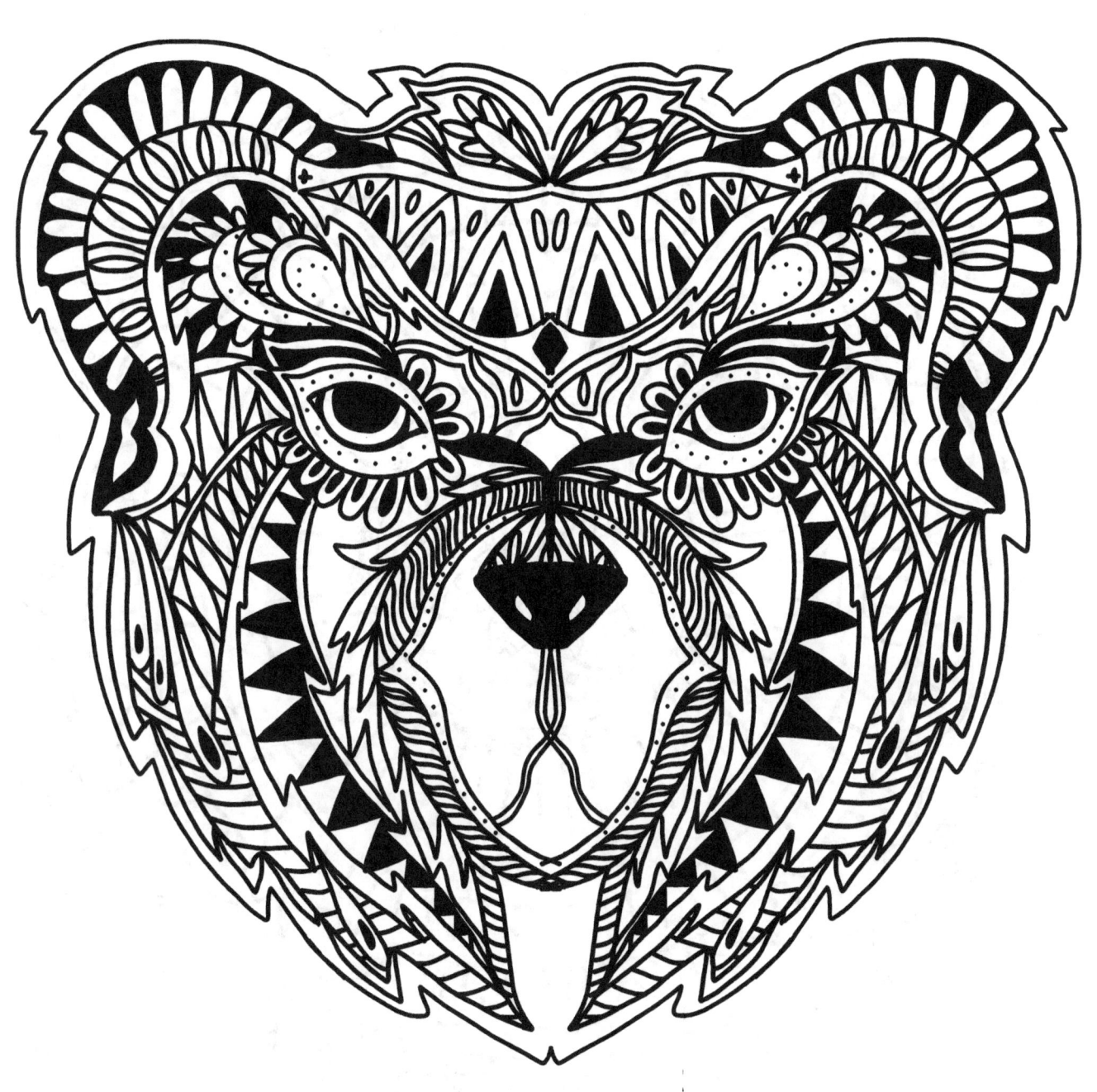

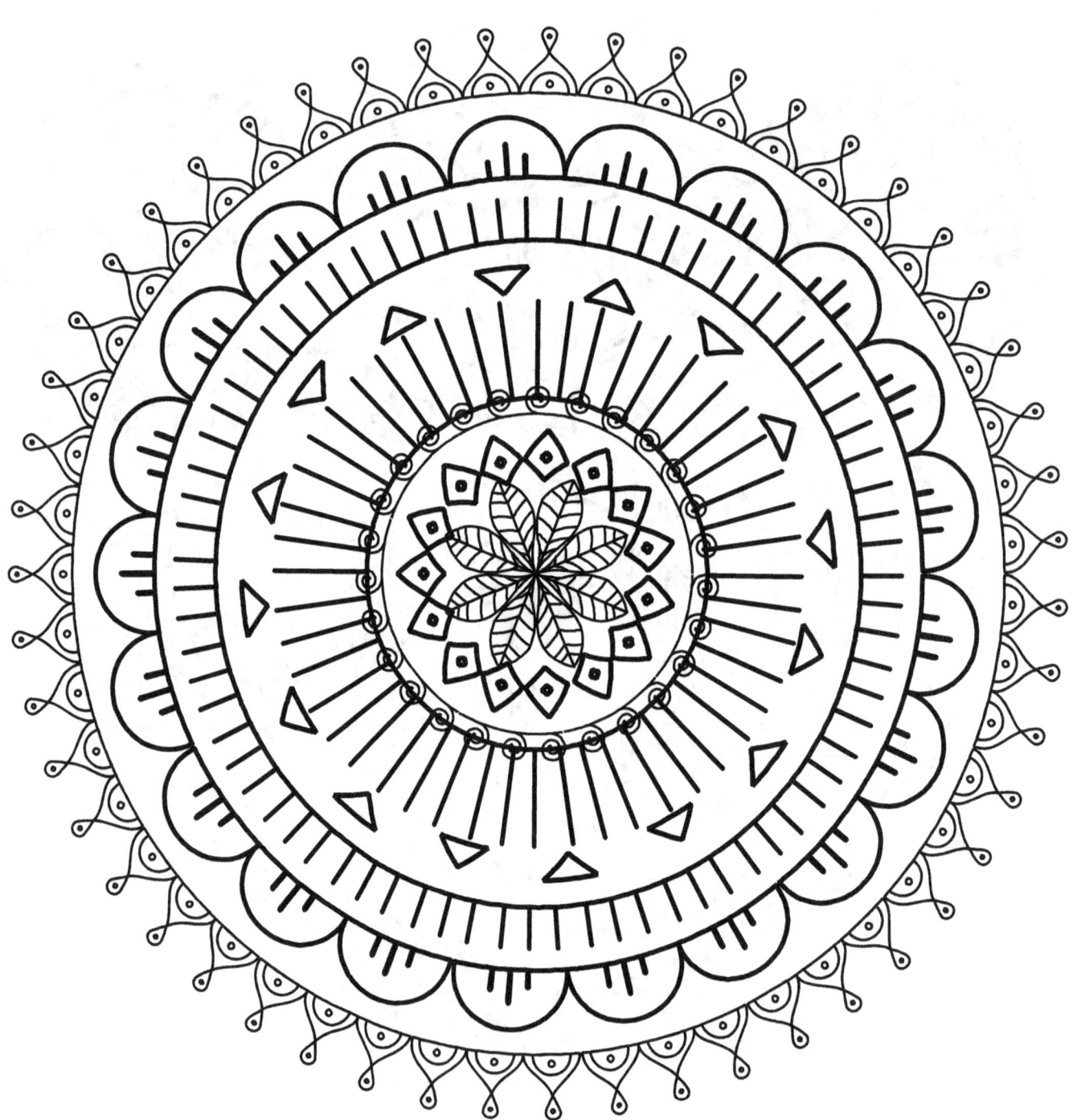

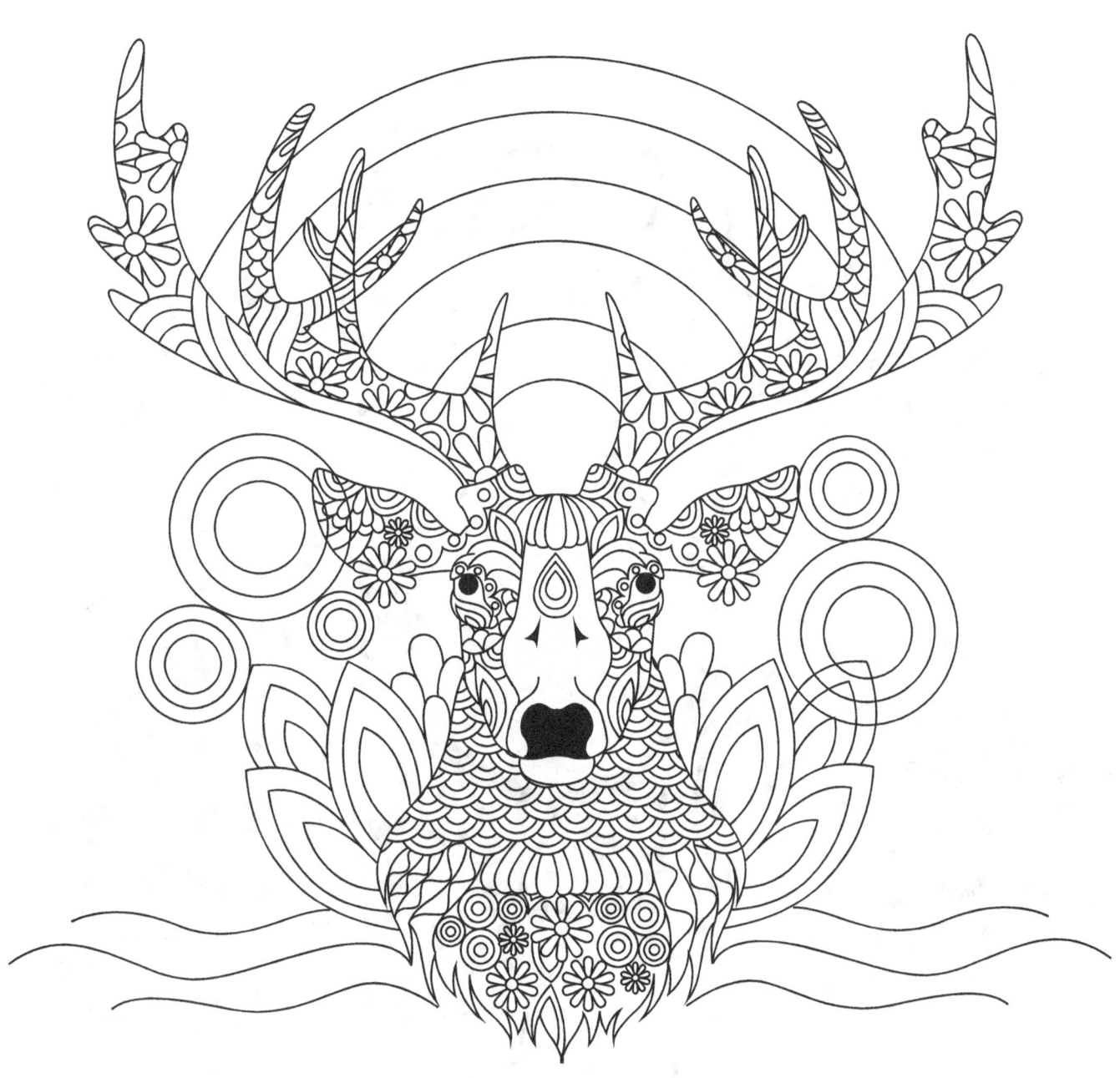

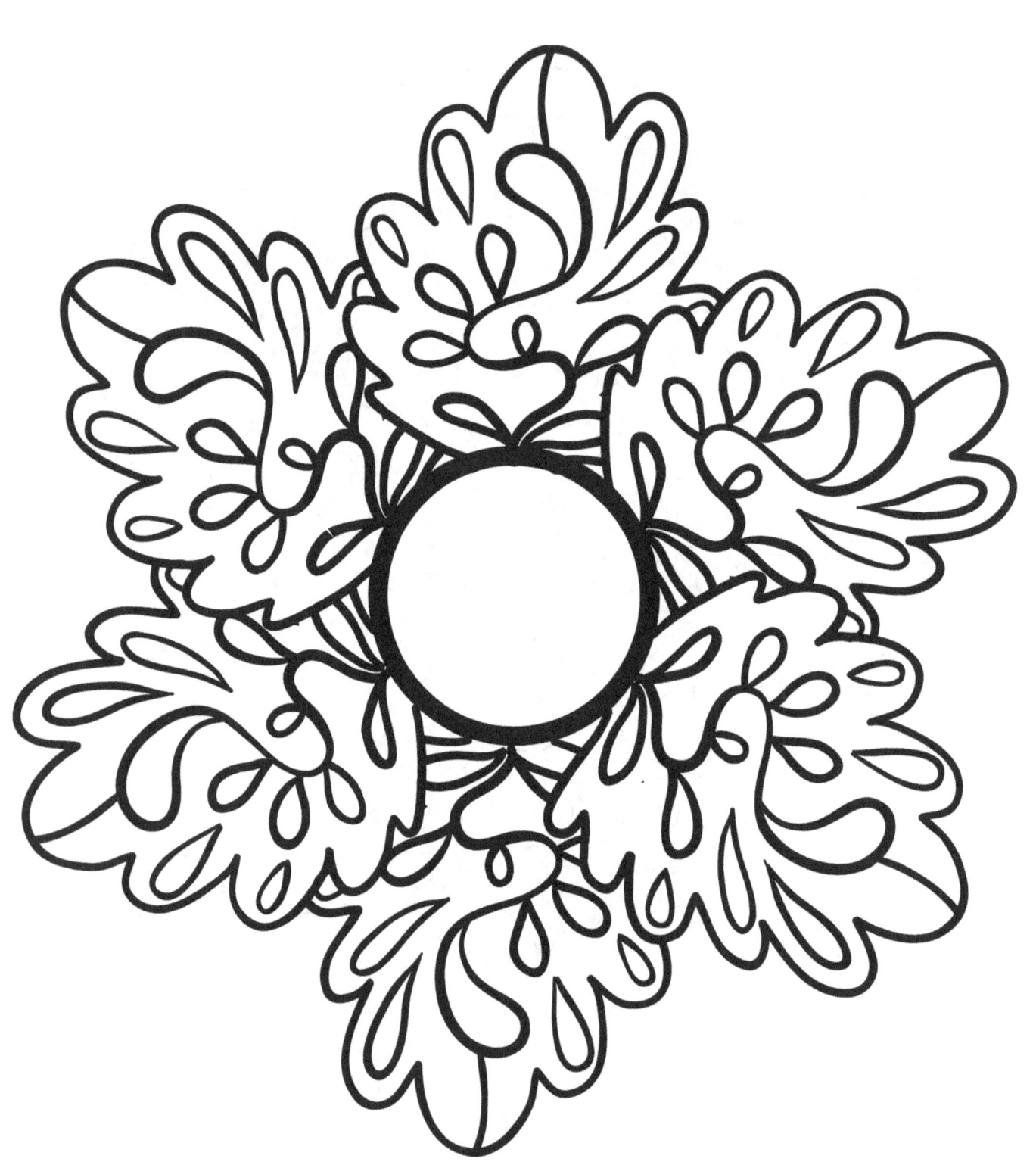

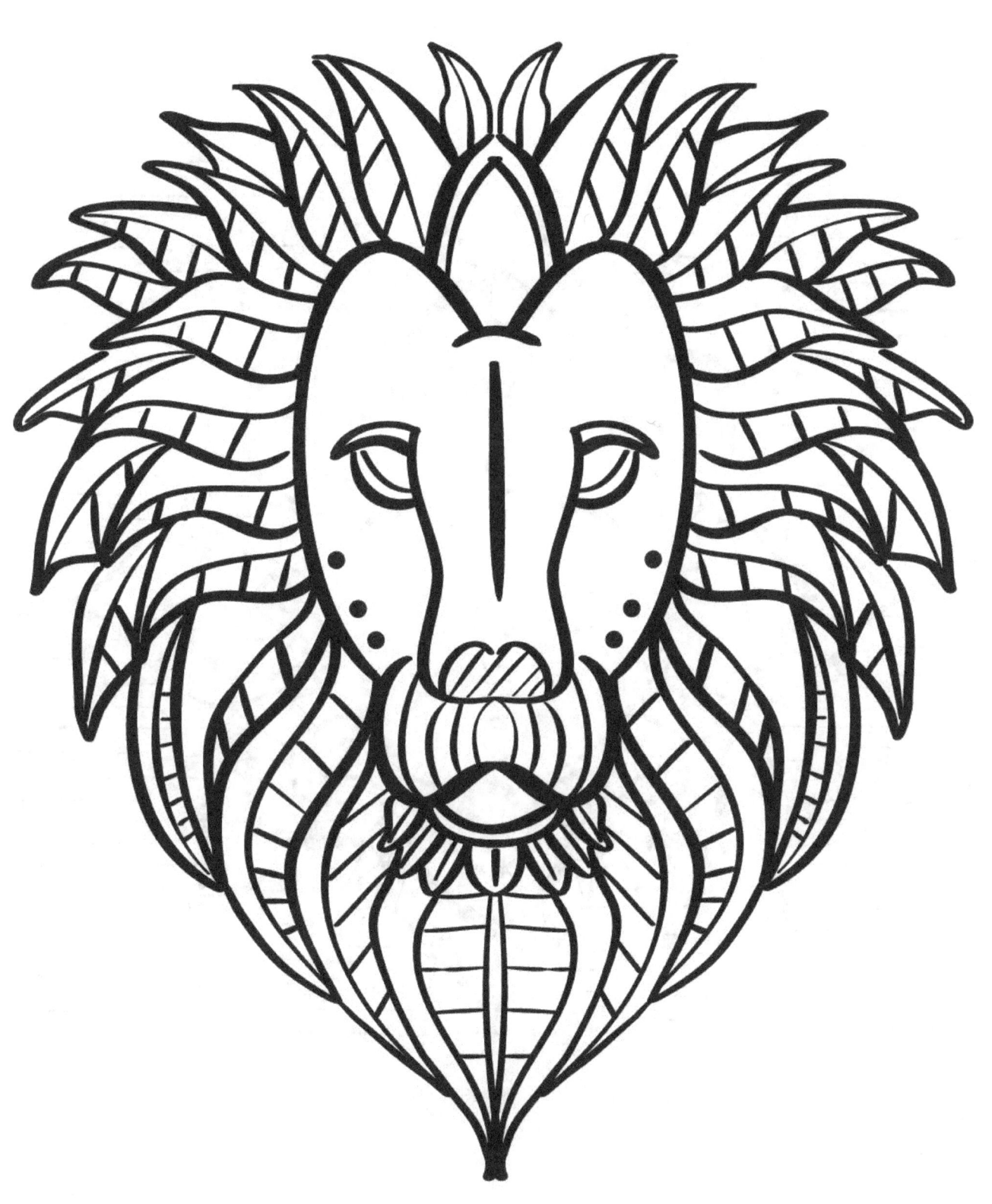

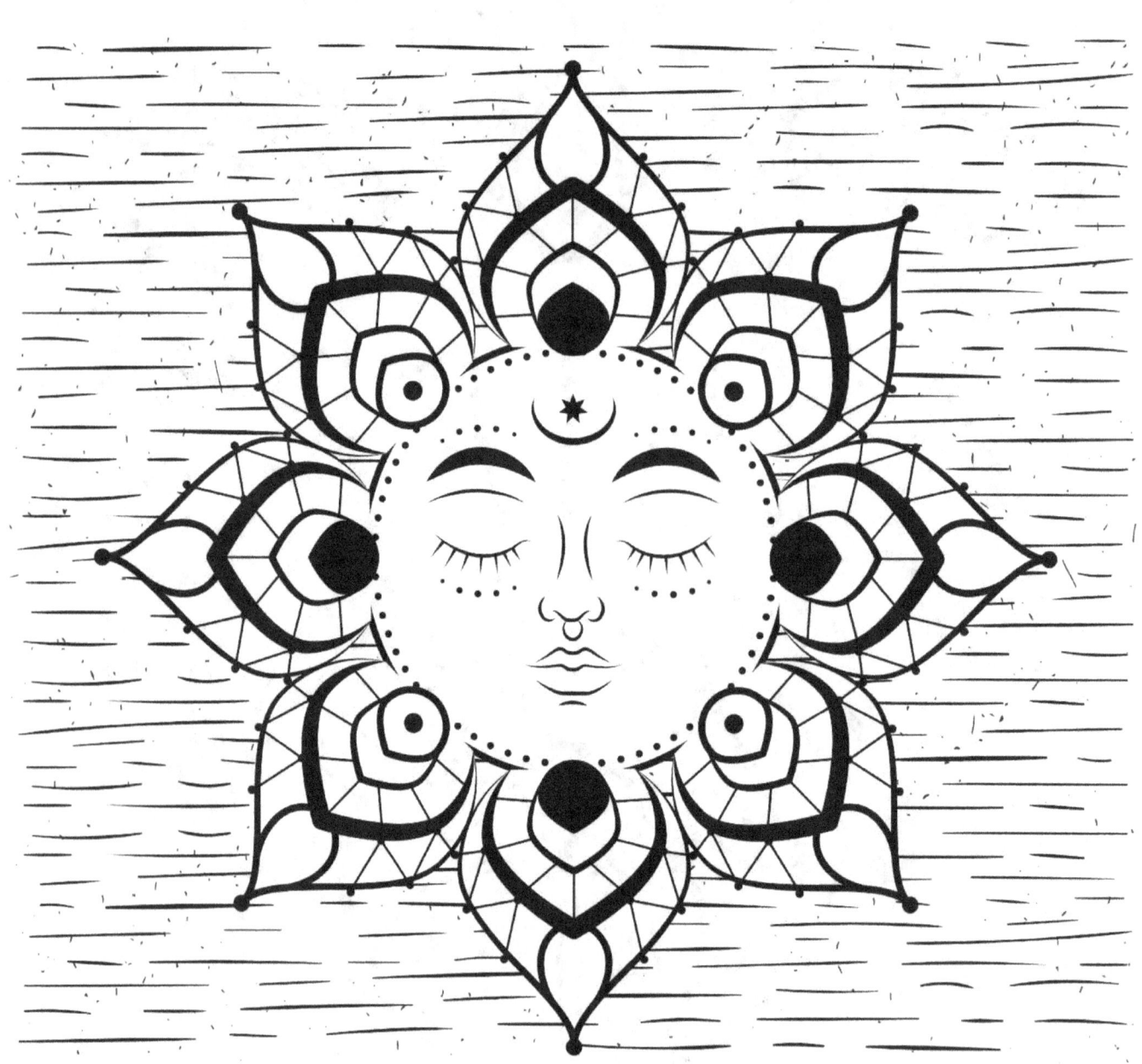

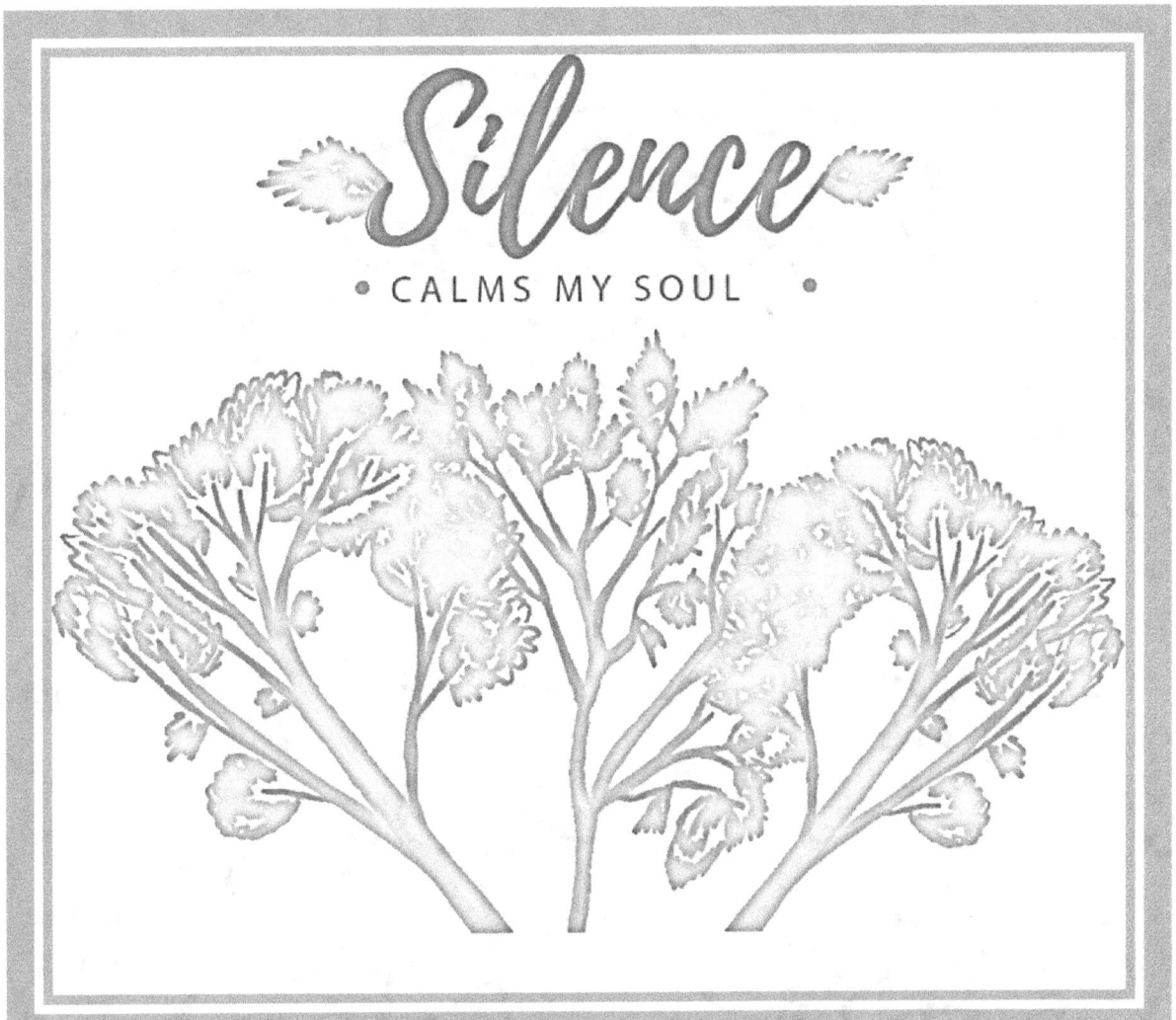

Note :
_____
_____
_____
_____
_____
_____

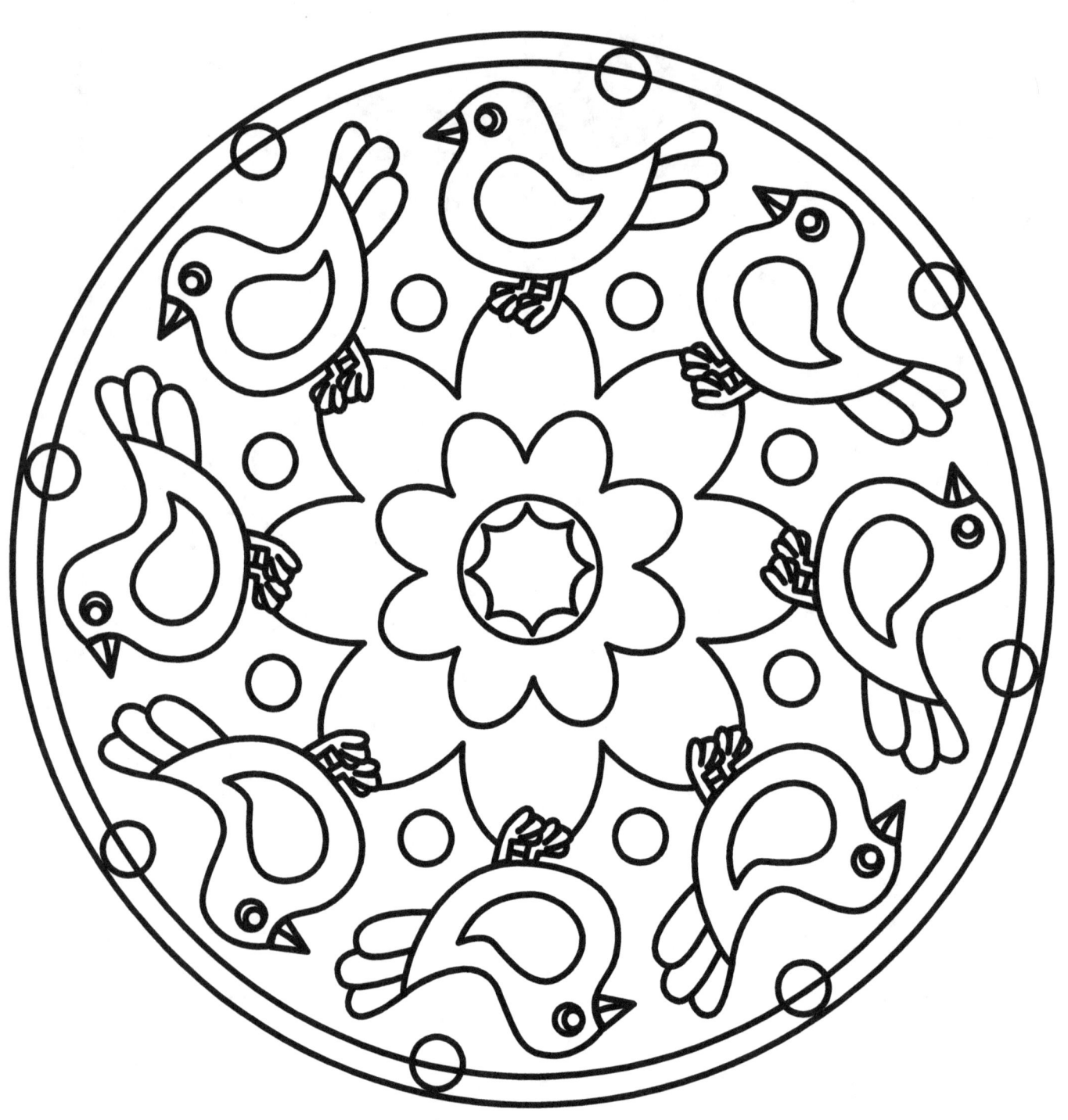

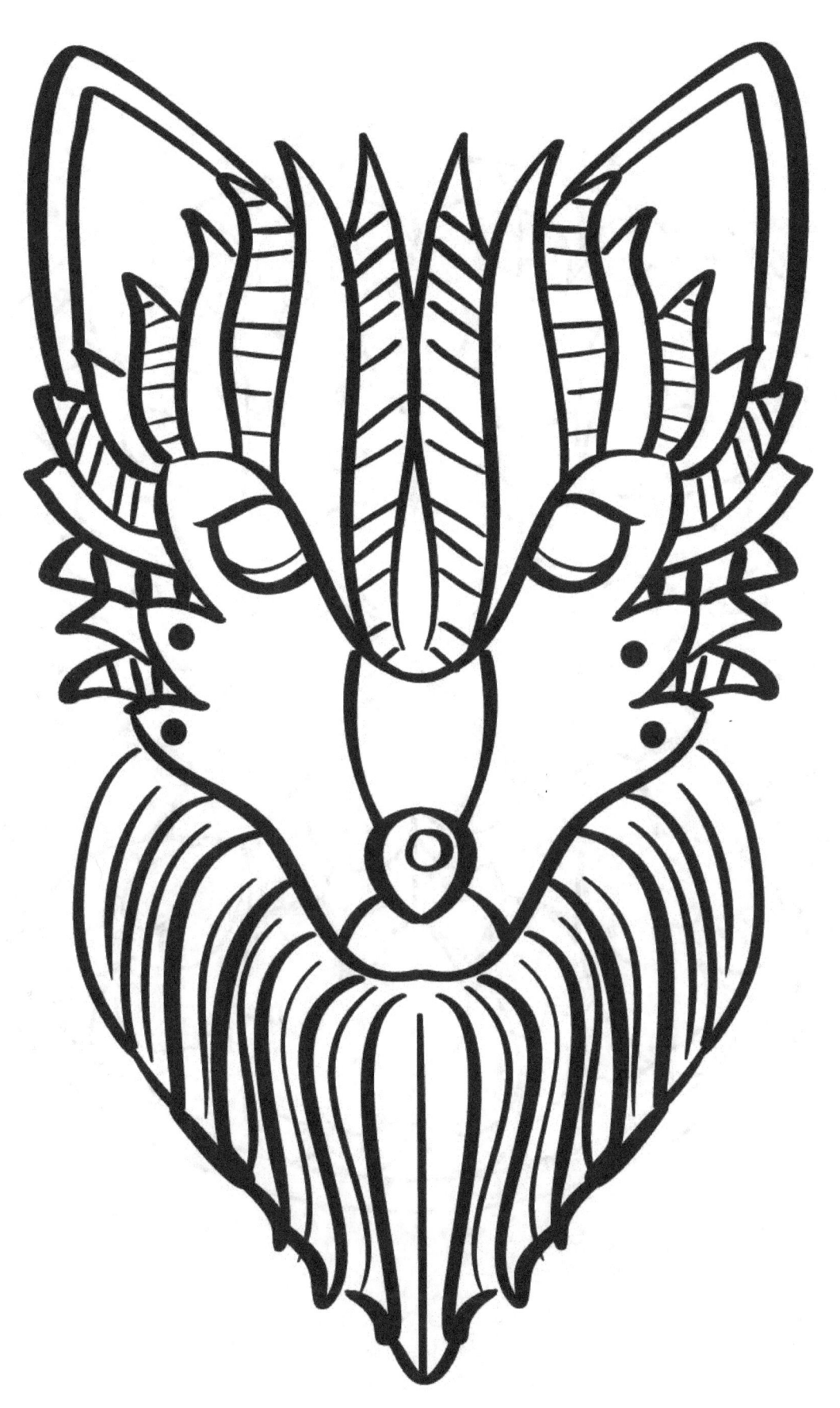

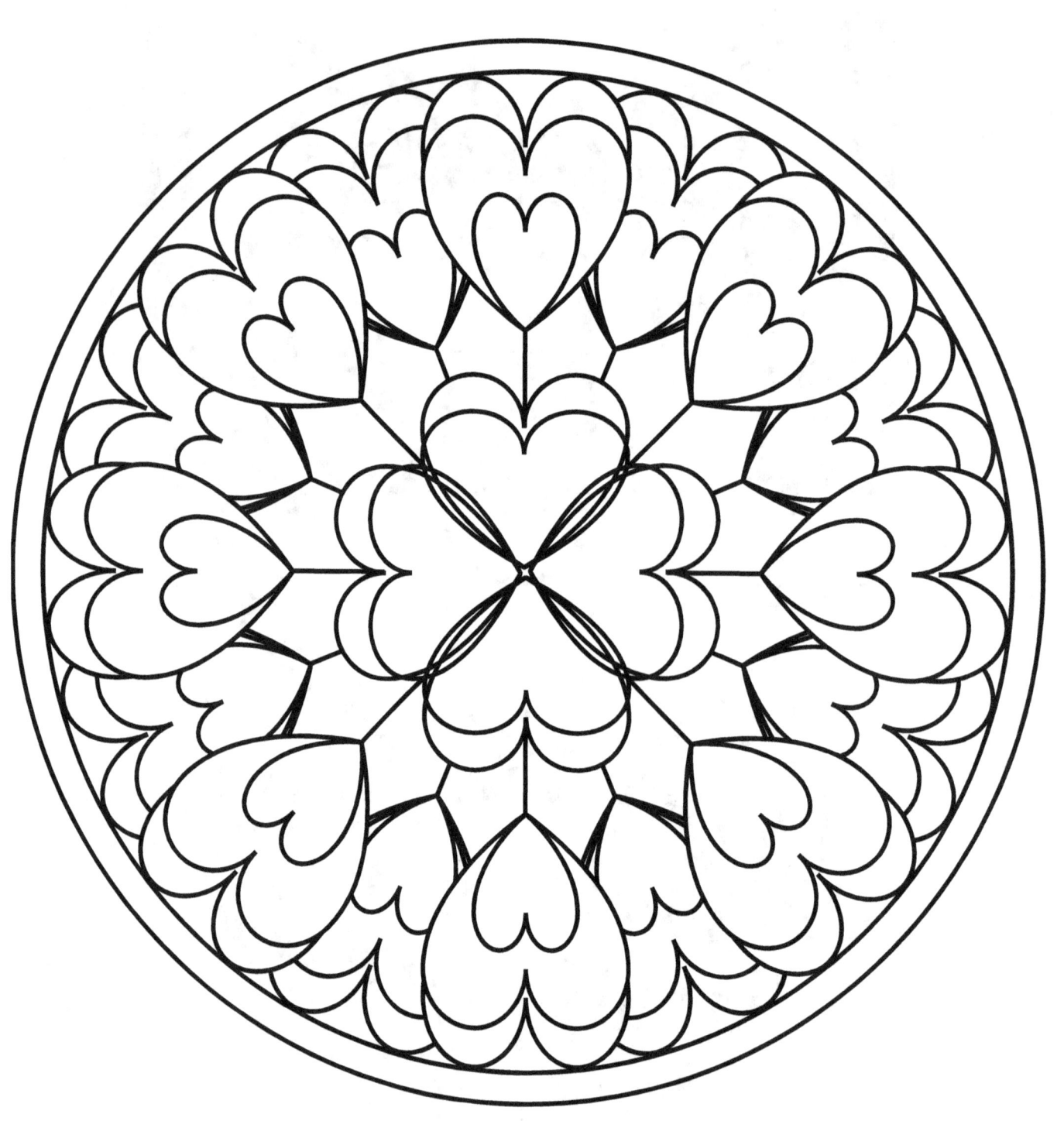

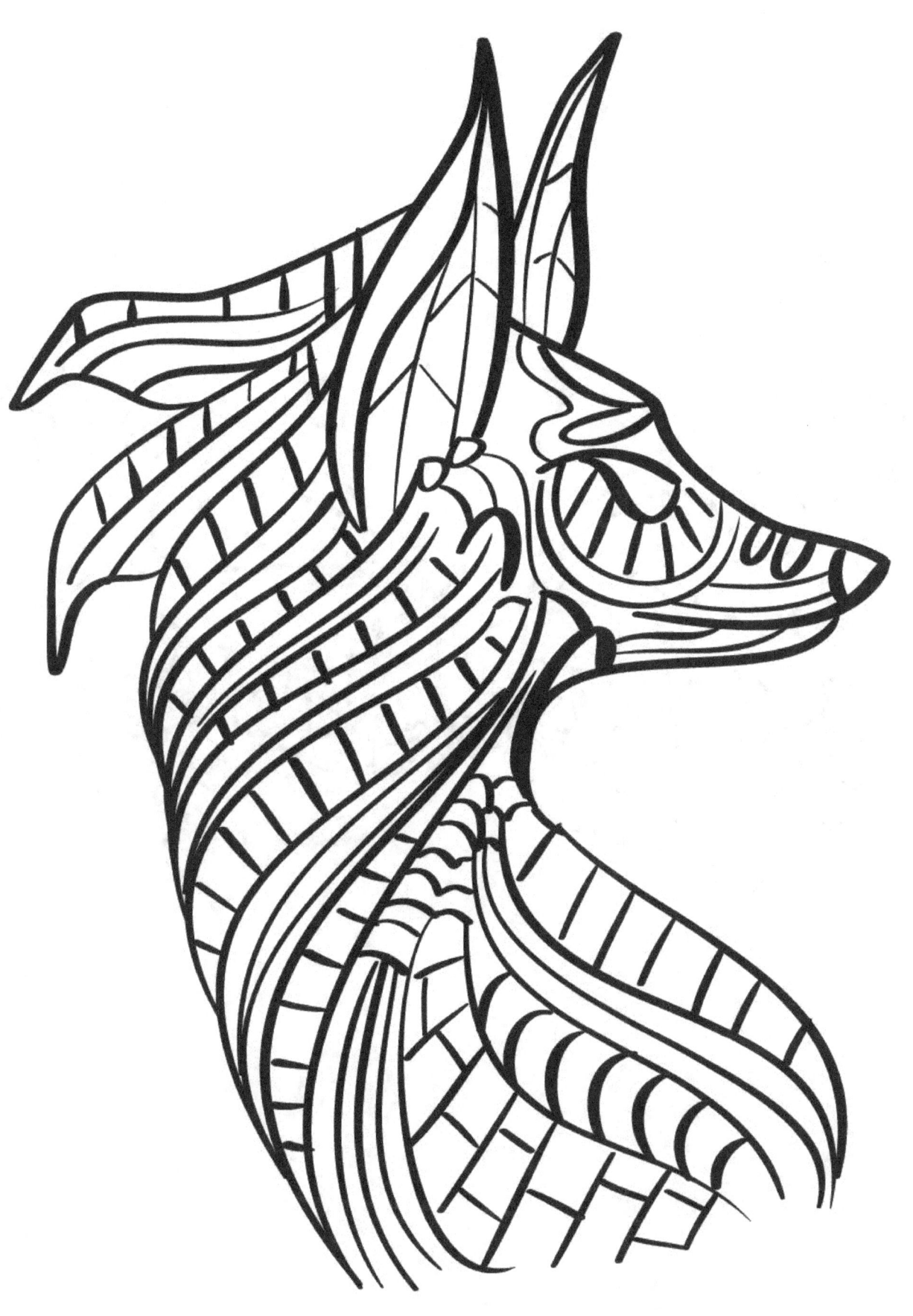

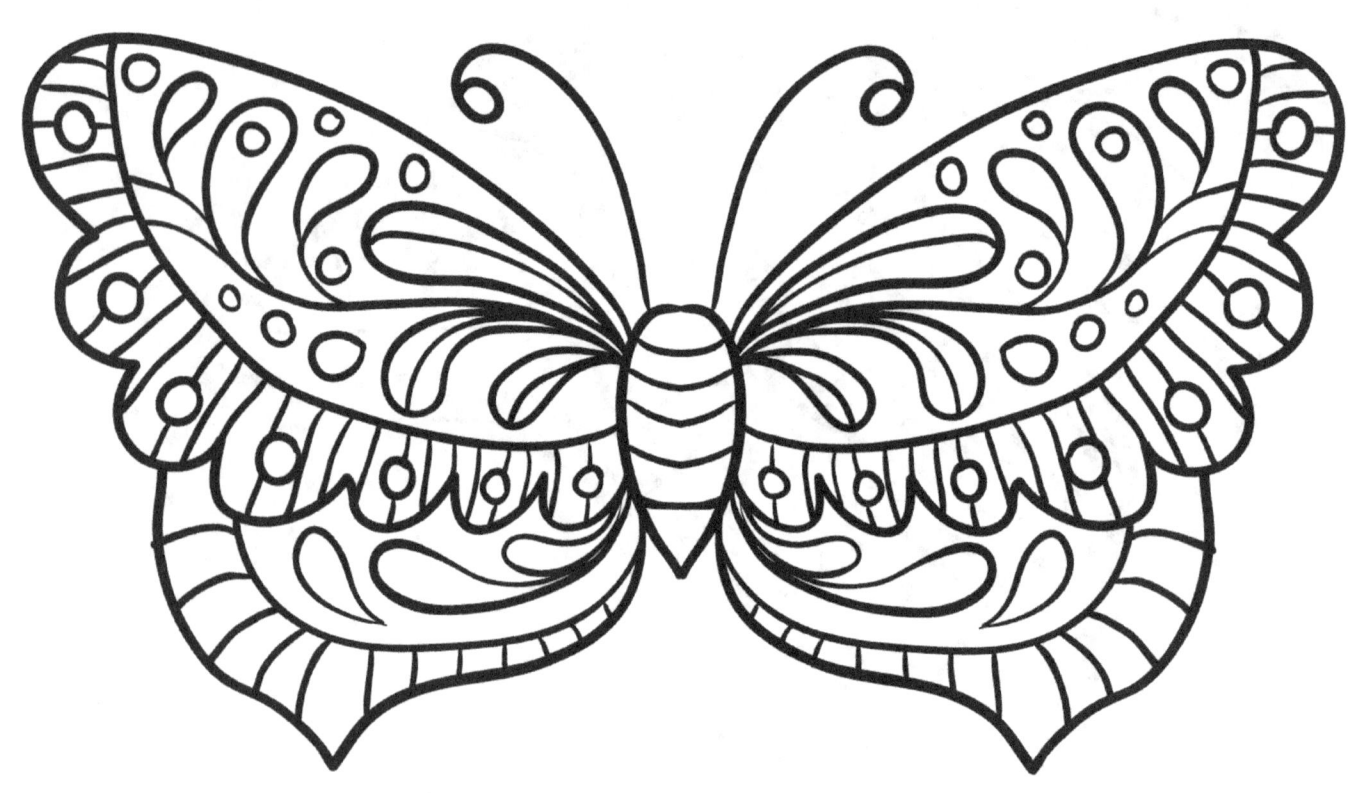

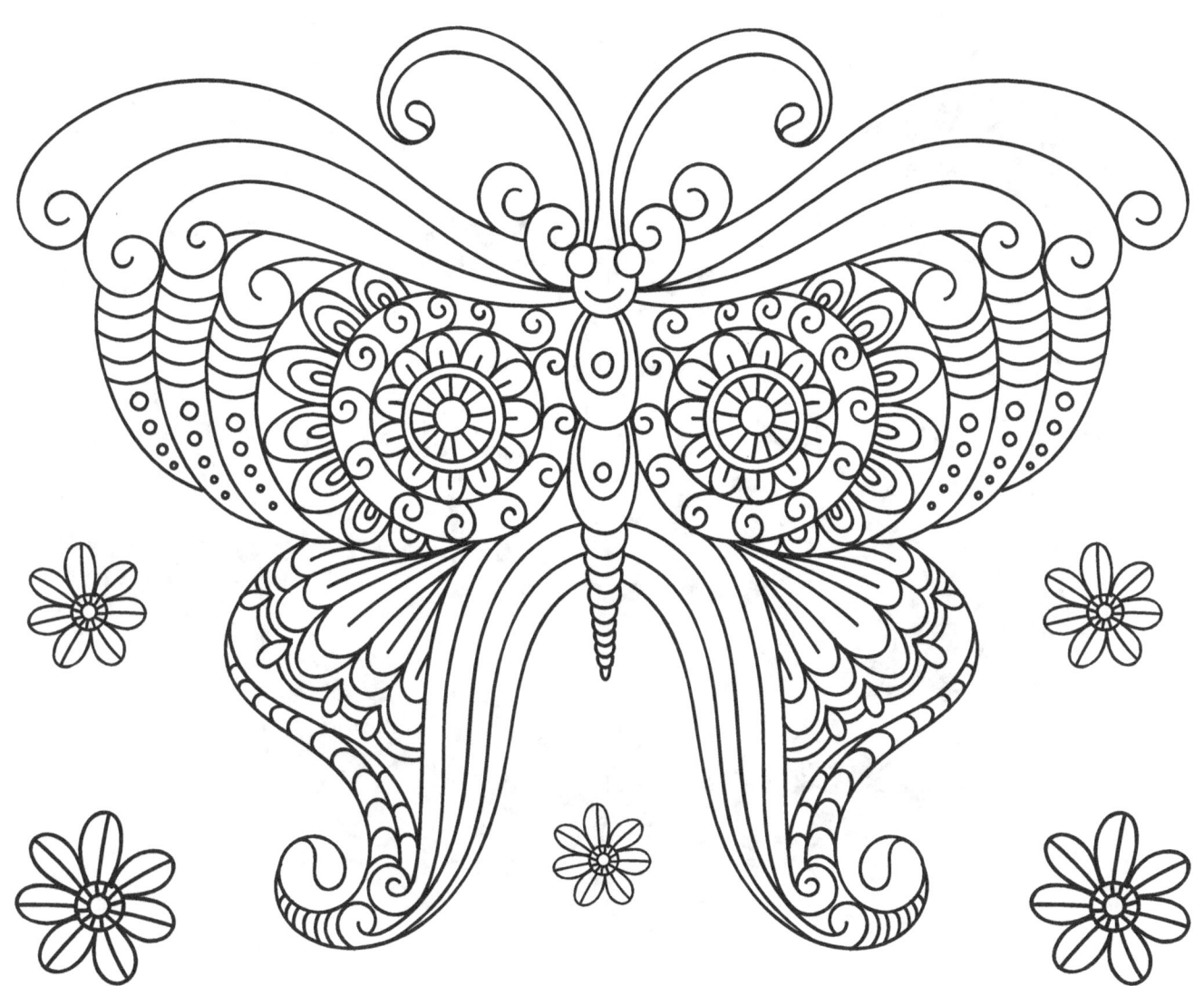

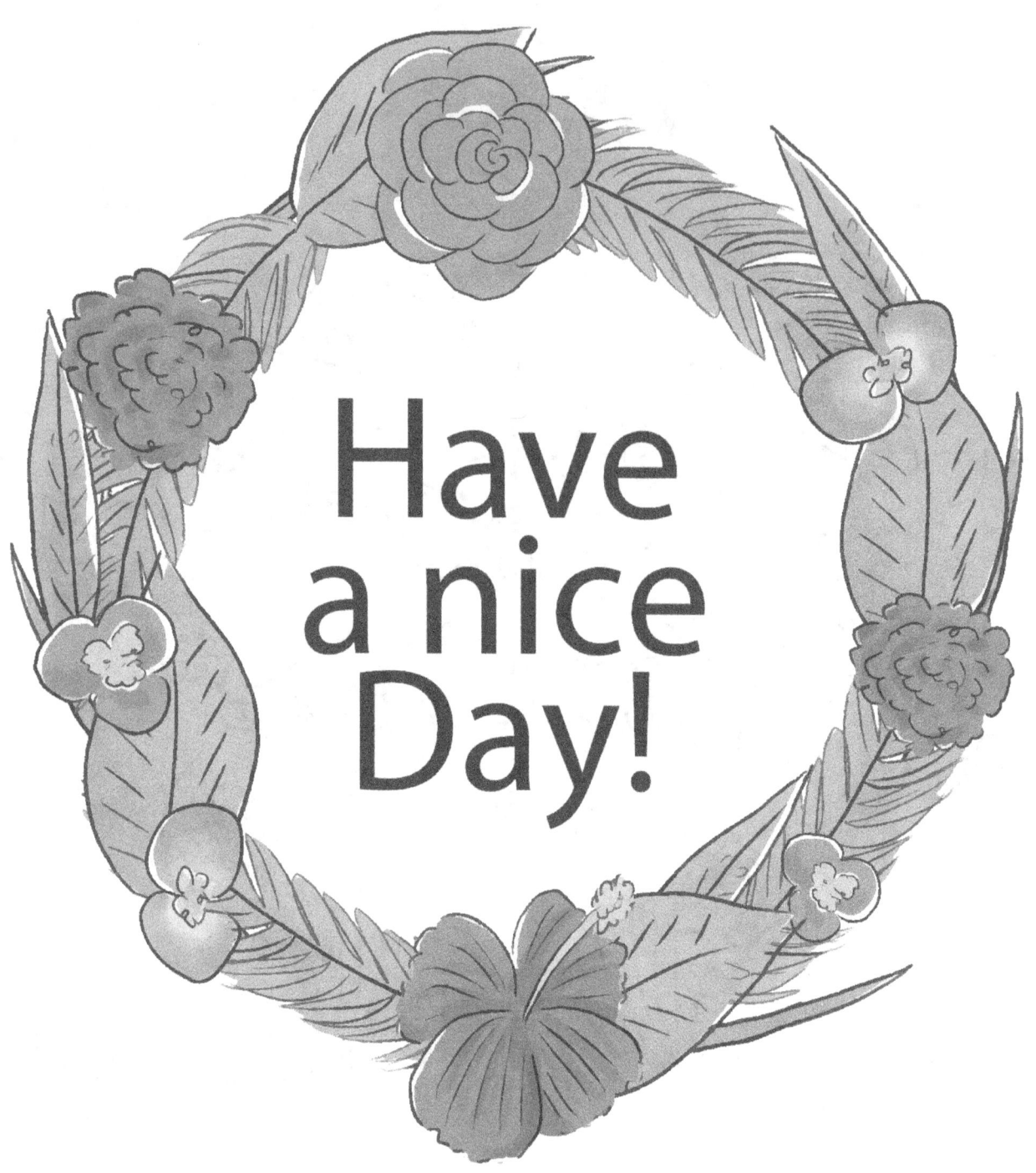

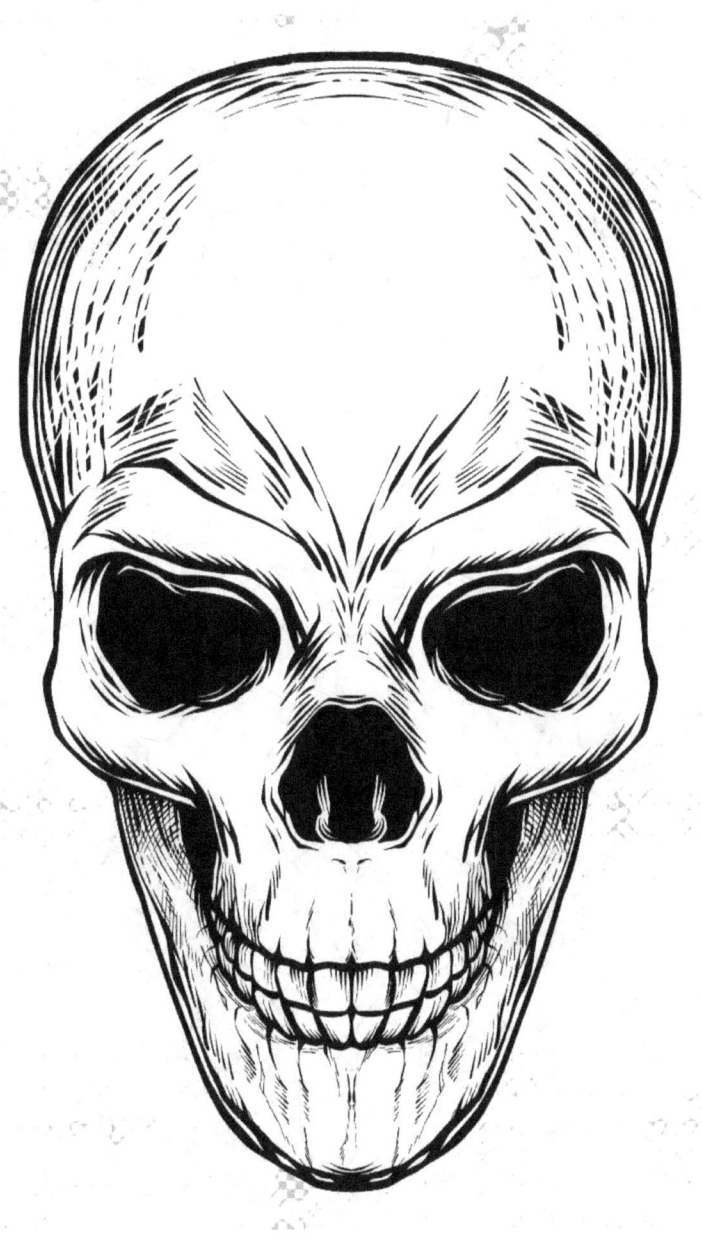

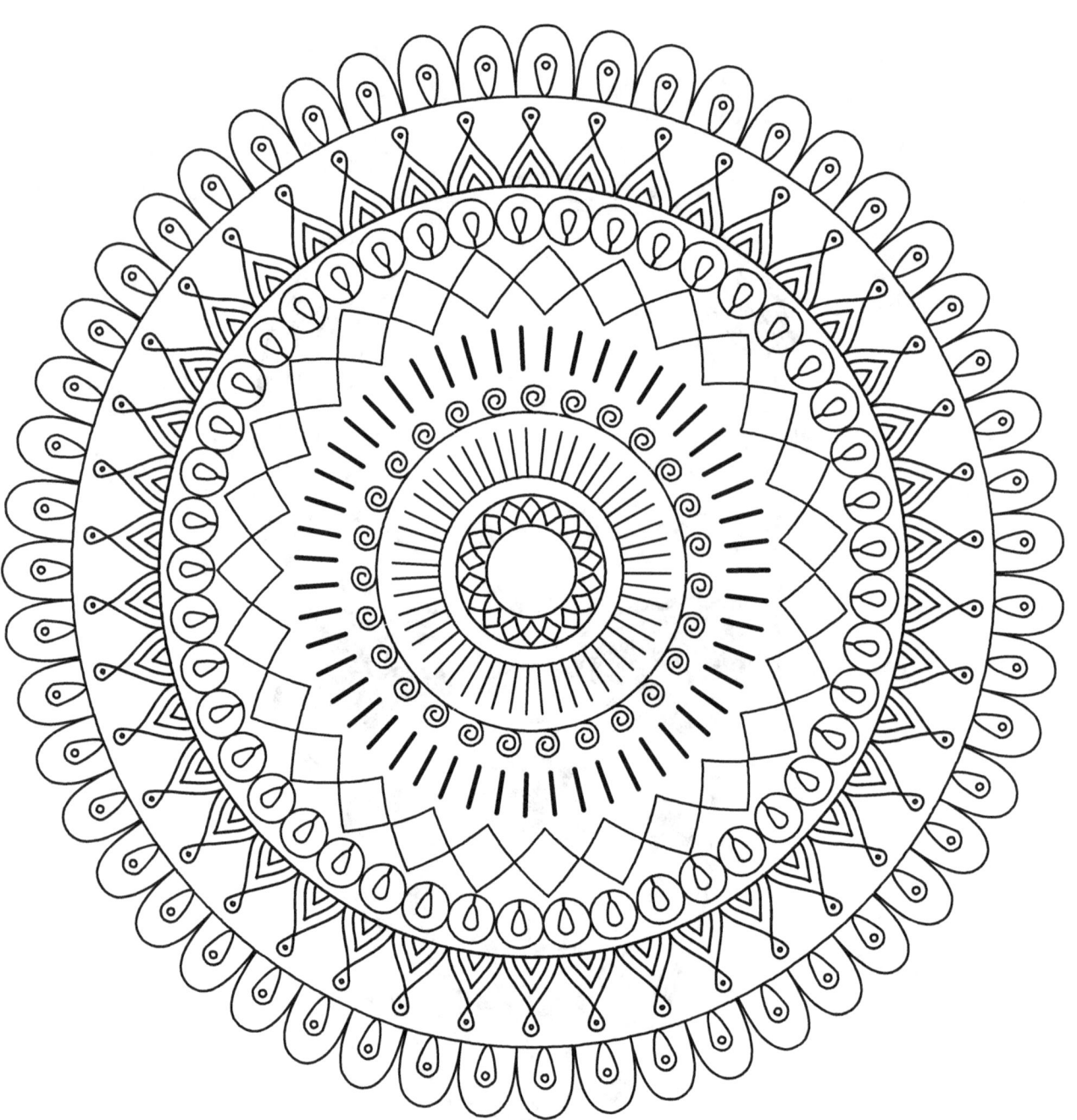

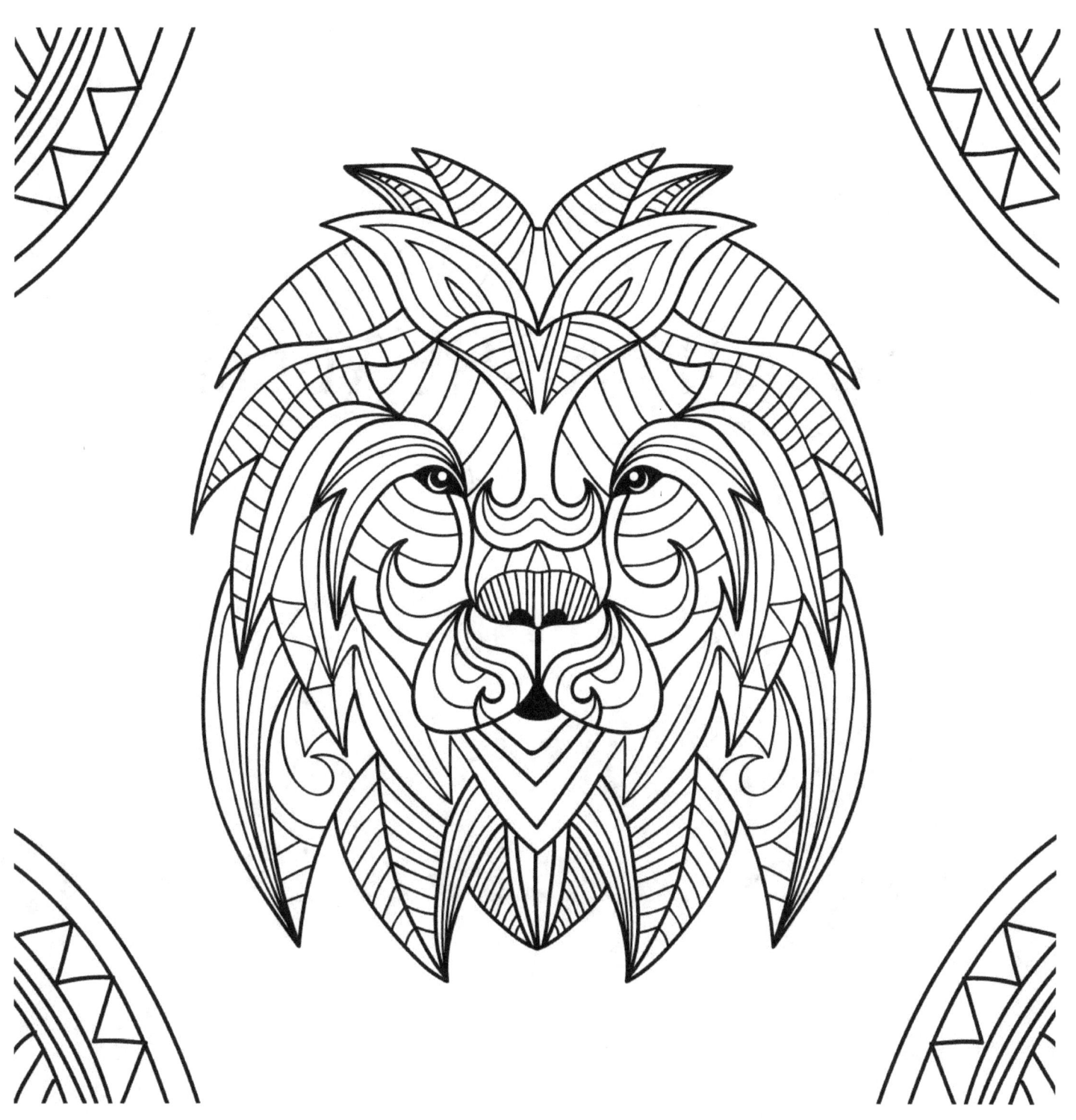

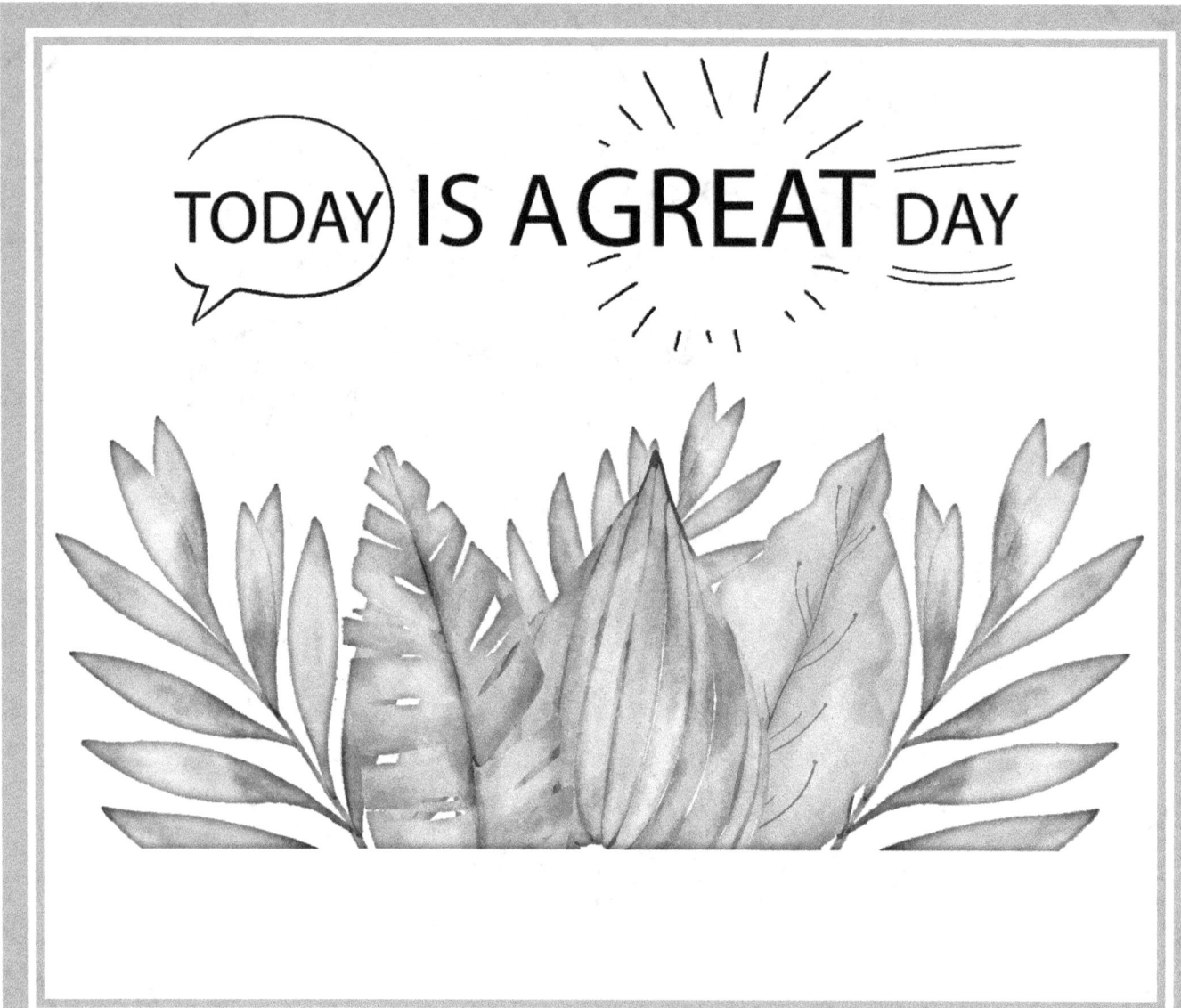

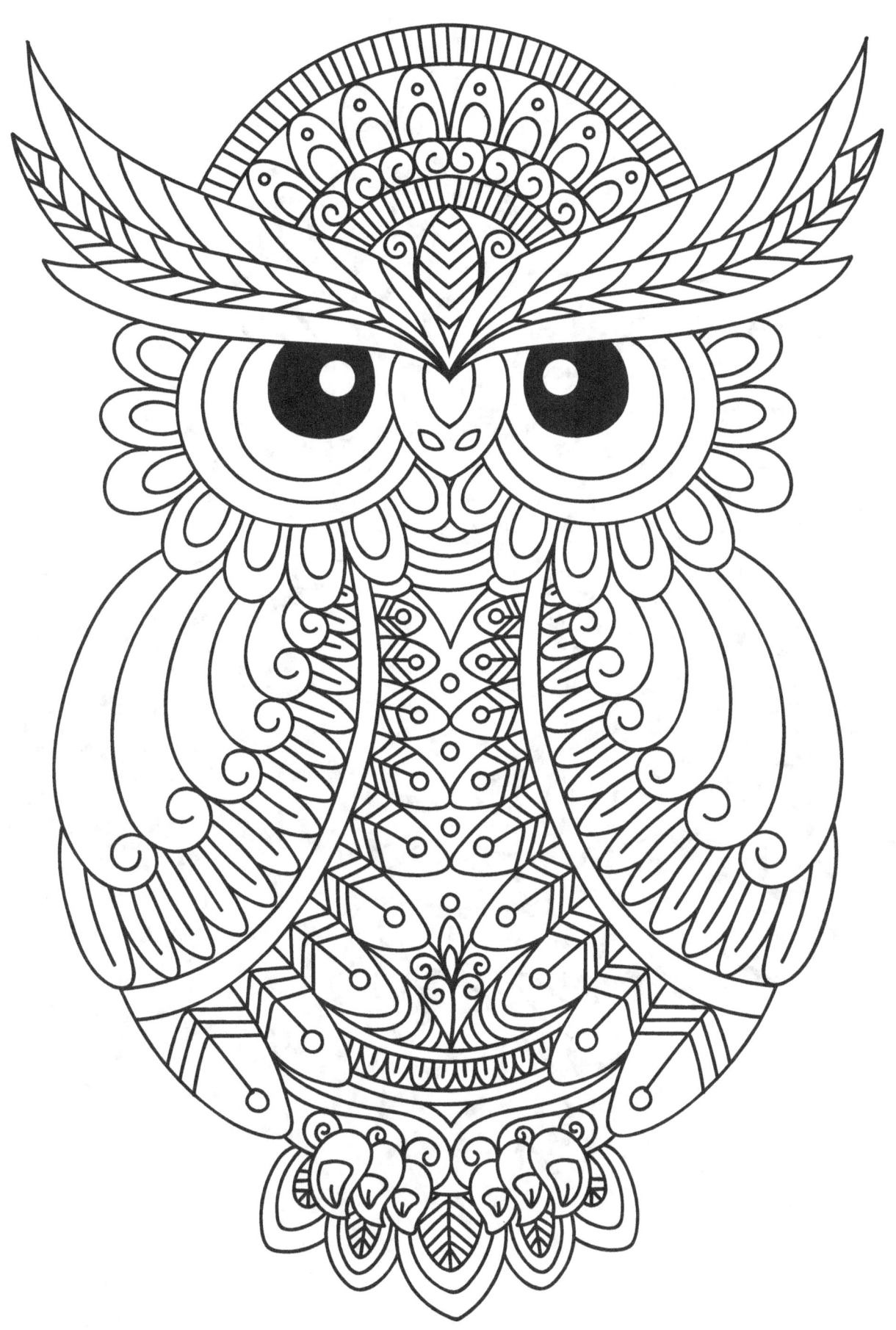

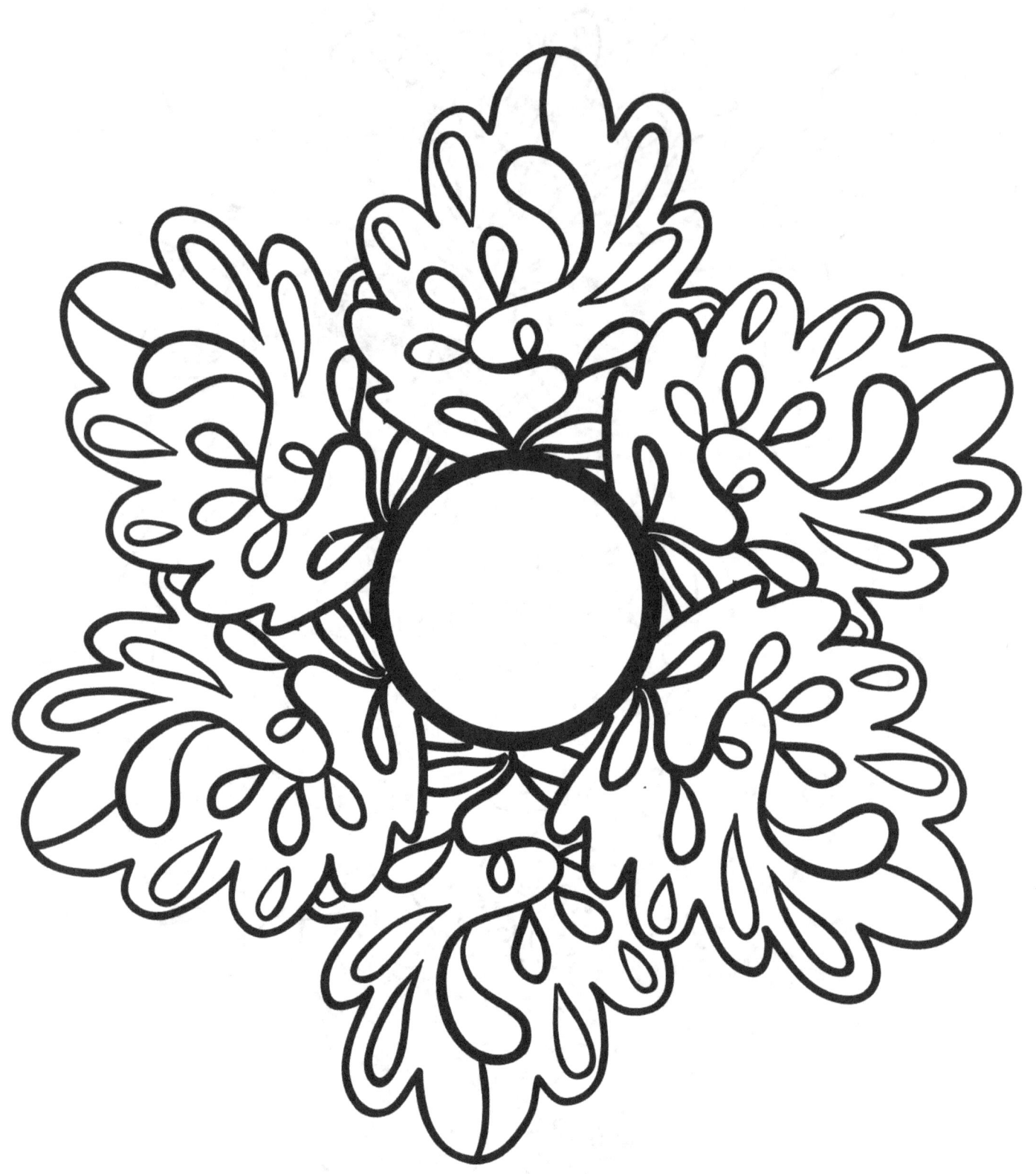

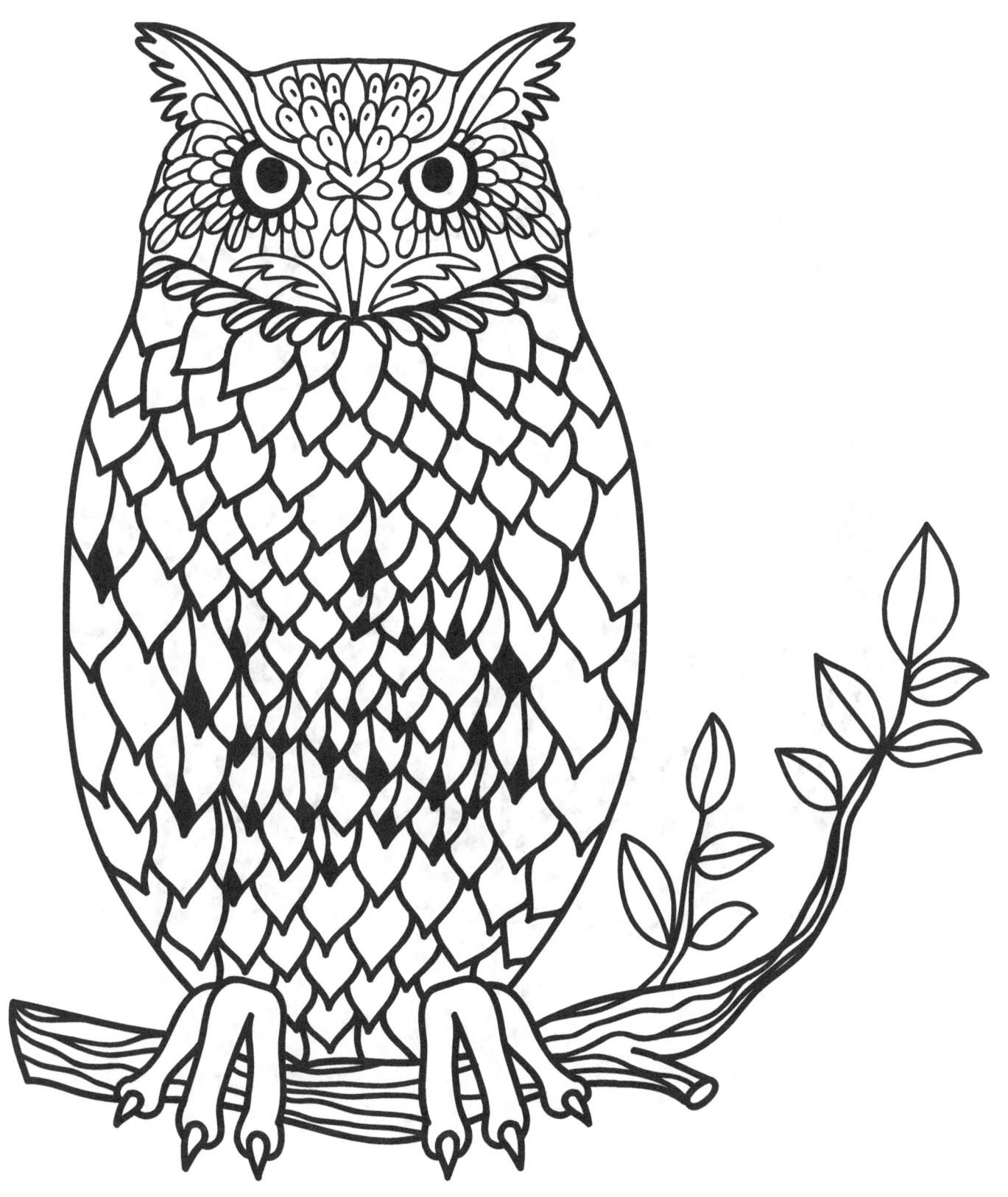

"A strong woman stands up for herself. A stronger woman stands up for every body else"

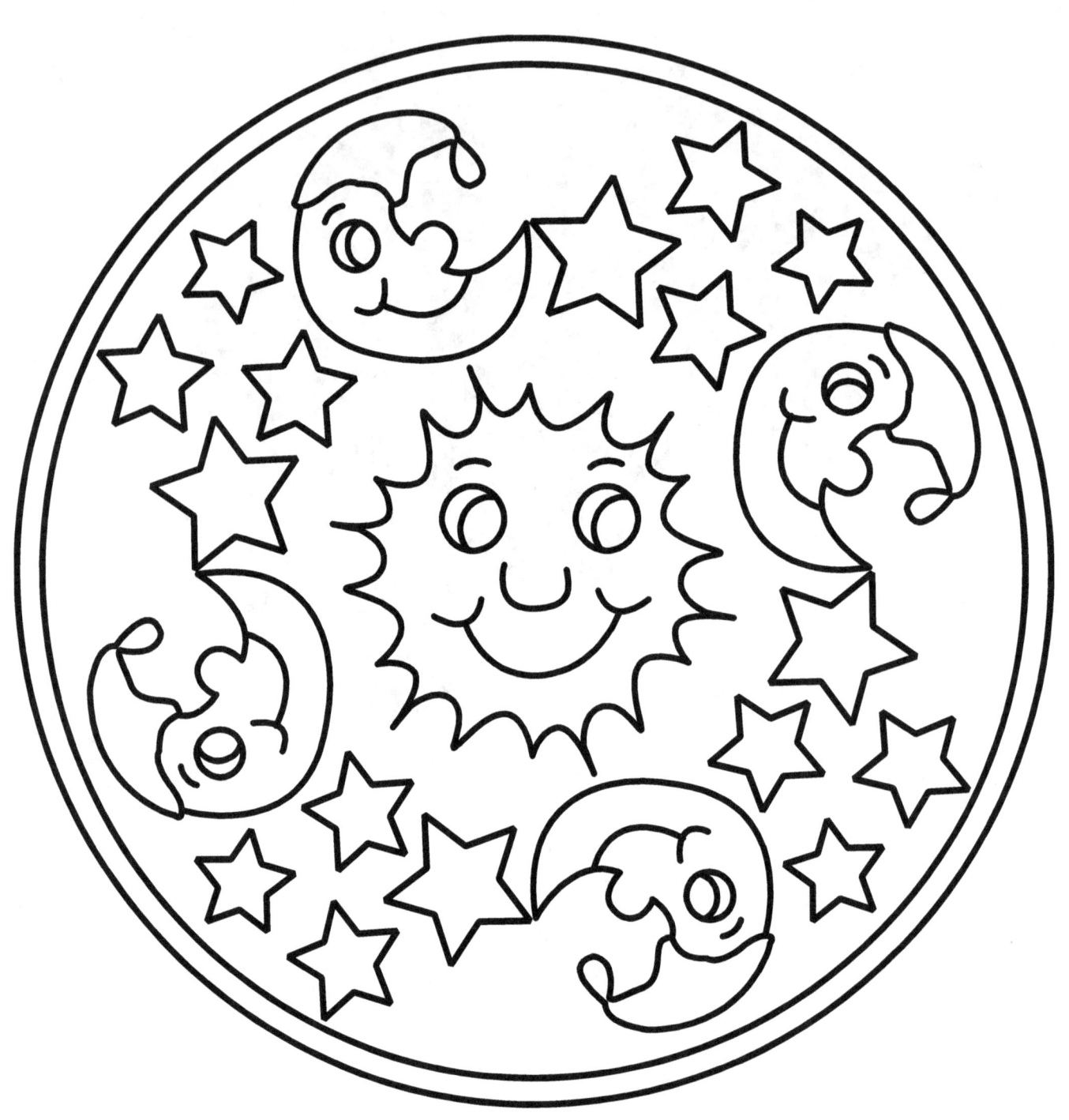

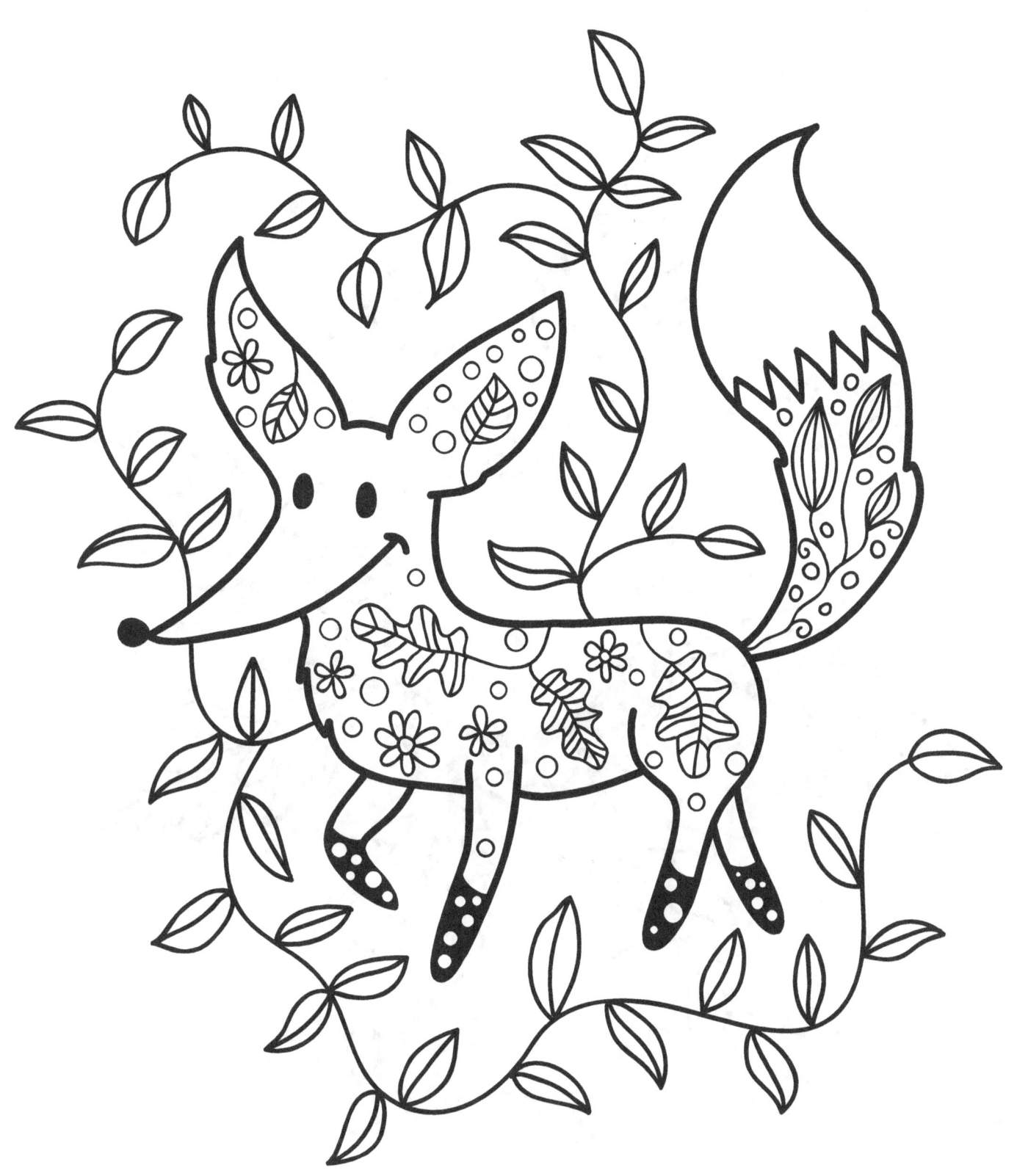

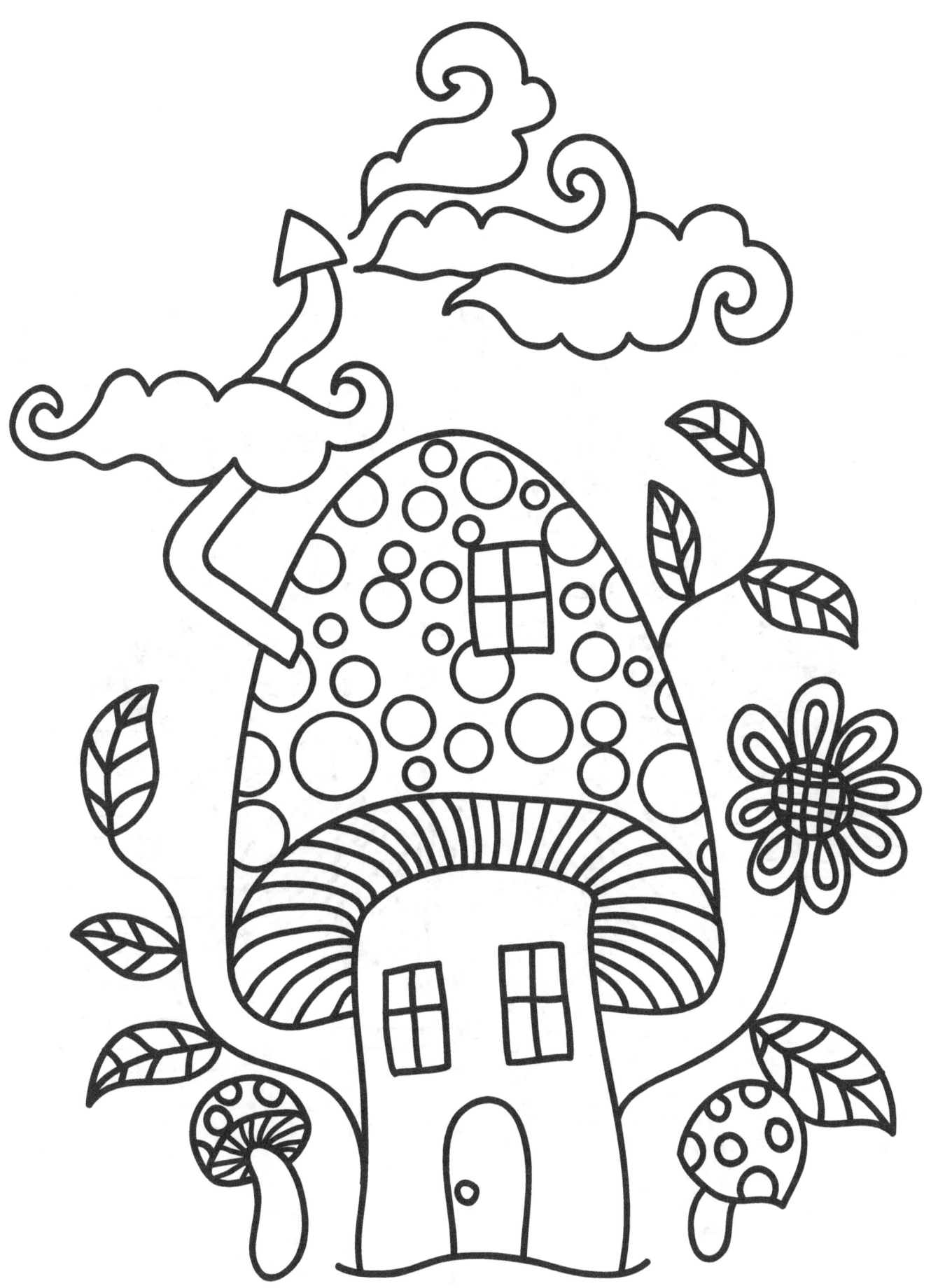

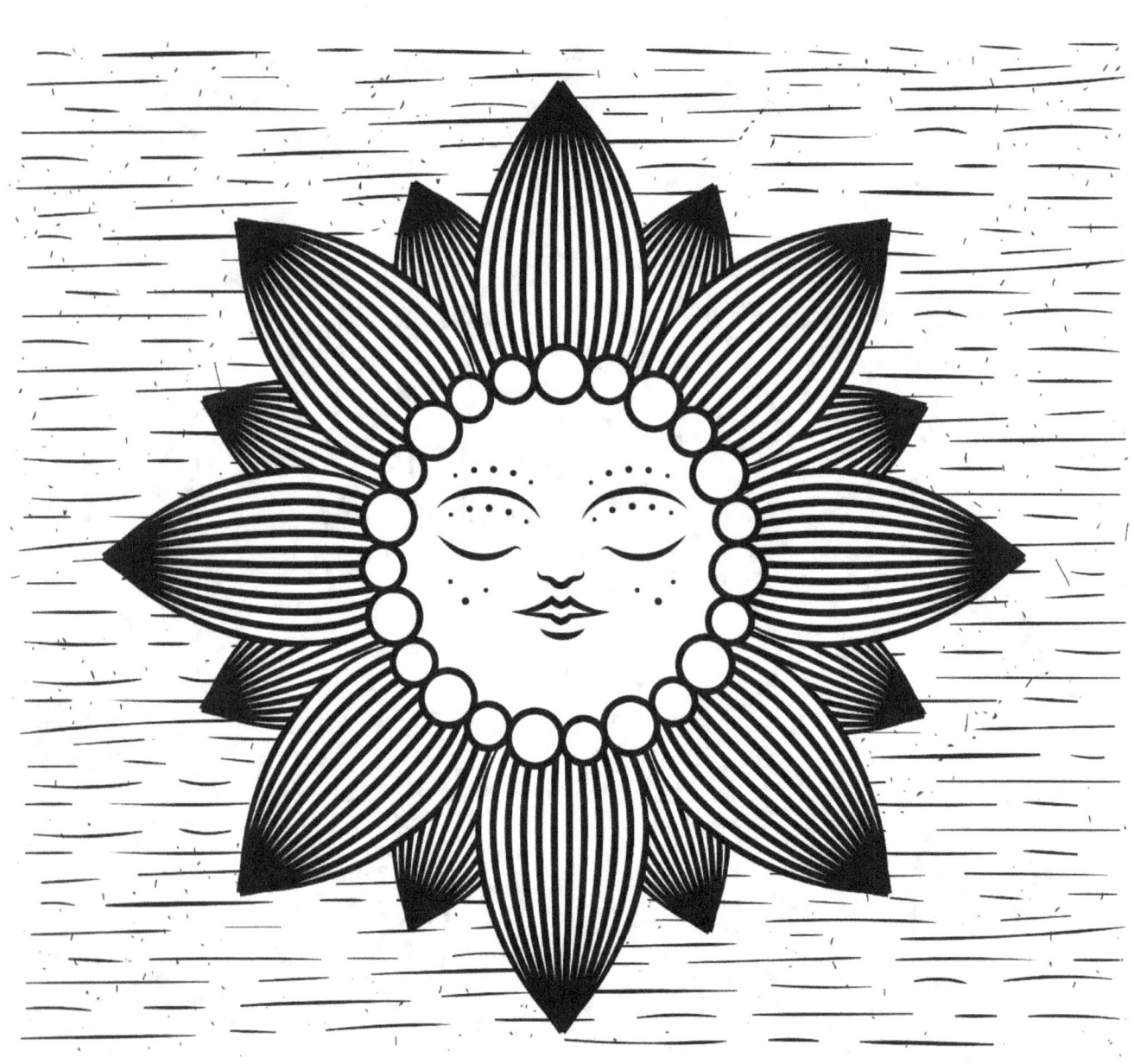

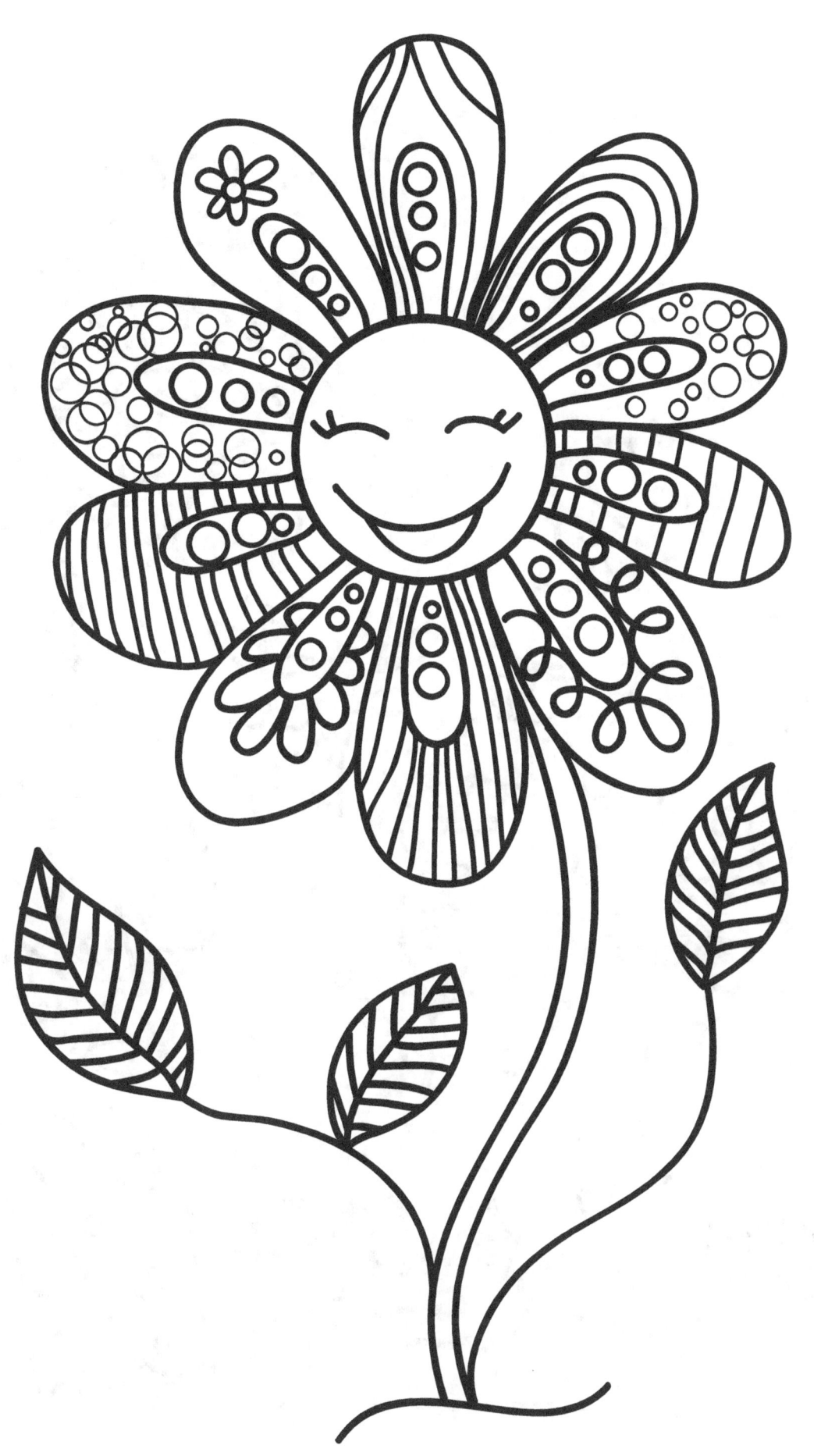

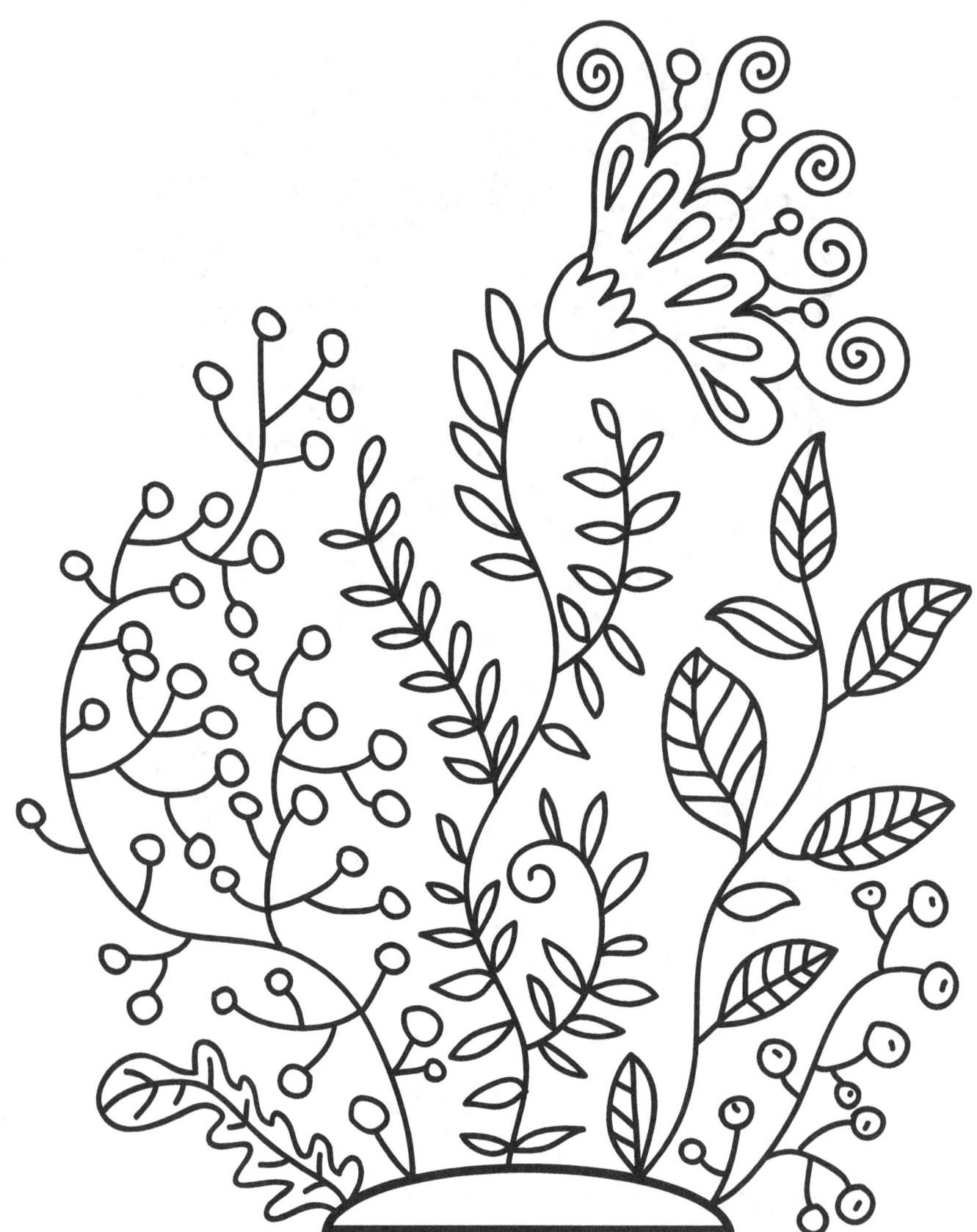

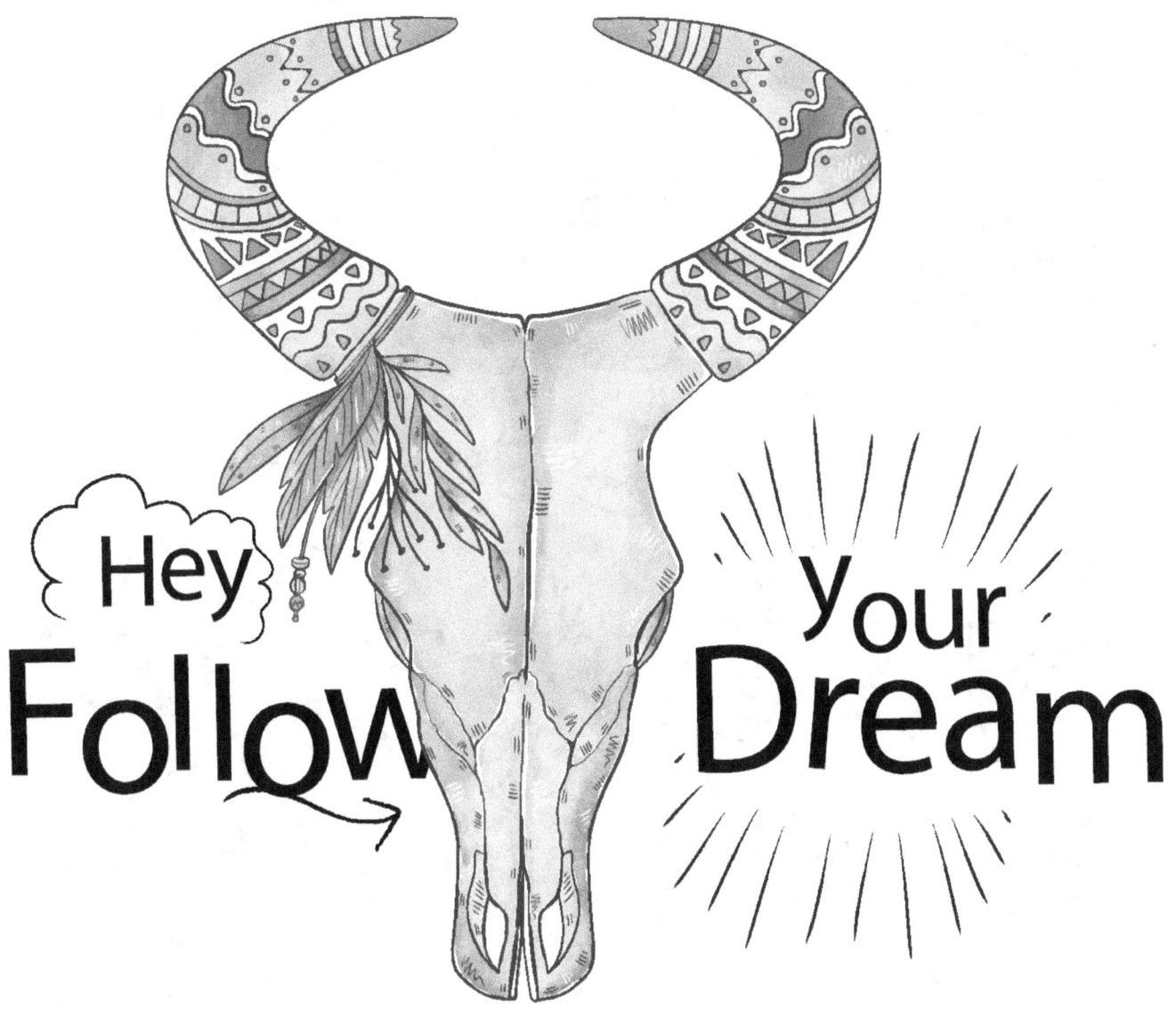

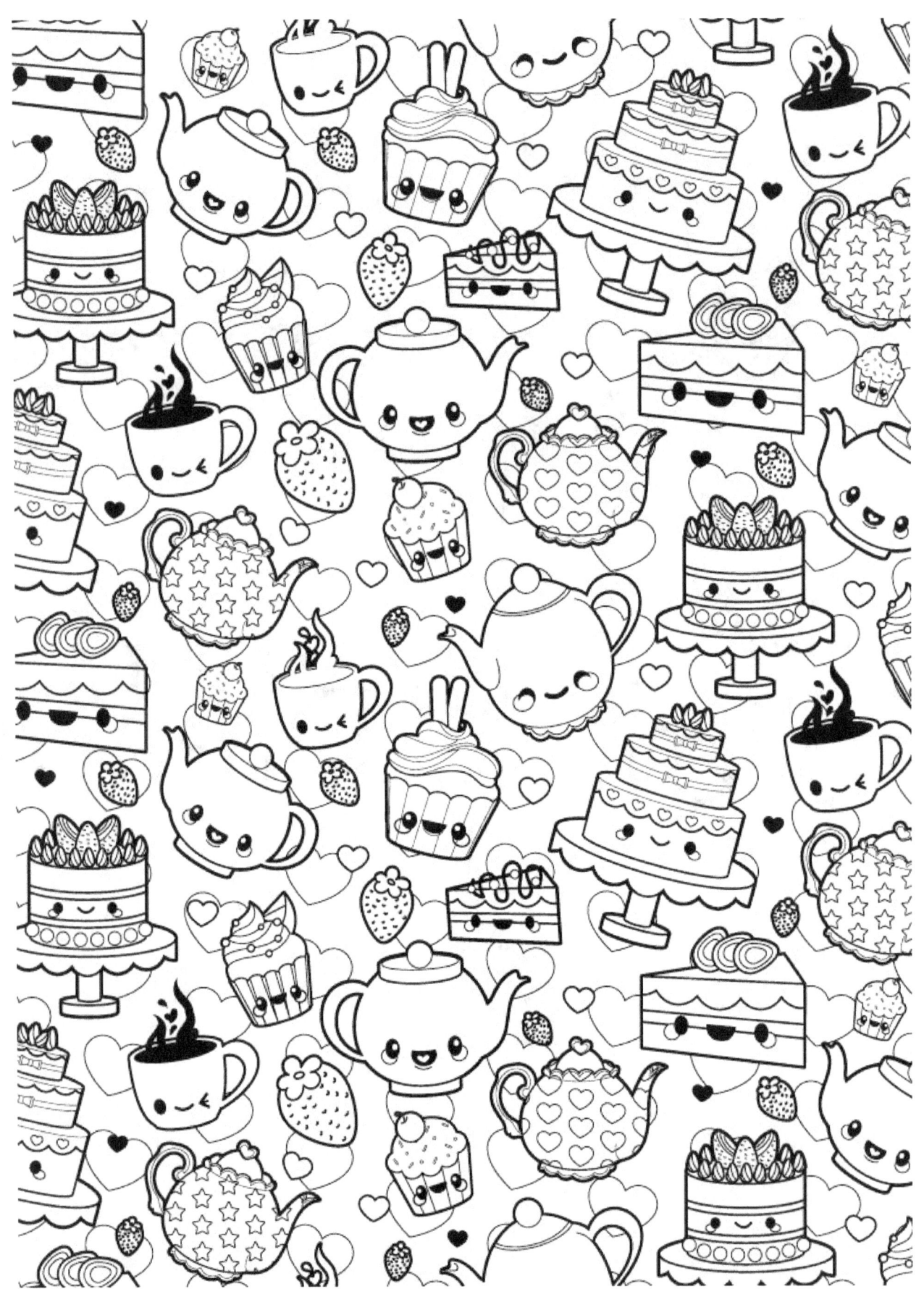